TACTICAL URBANISM FOR LIBRARIANS

TACTICAL URBANISM FOR LIBRARIANS

Quick, Low-Cost Ways to Make Big Changes

KAREN MUNRO

An imprint of the American Library Association
CHICAGO 2017

KAREN MUNRO is head of the University of Oregon Portland Library and Learning Commons. Previously she was e-learning librarian at the University of California, Berkeley and literature librarian at the University of Oregon. She has an MFA from the University of Iowa Writers' Workshop and an MLIS from the University of British Columbia. She publishes and presents often on topics related to library design and outreach to users, particularly those in the fields of architecture and design.

© 2017 by Karen Munro

Extensive effort has gone into ensuring the reliability of the information in this book; however, the publisher makes no warranty, express or implied, with respect to the material contained herein.

ISBNs
978-0-8389-1558-5 (paper)
978-0-8389-1584-4 (PDF)
978-0-8389-1585-1 (ePub)
978-0-8389-1586-8 (Kindle)

Library of Congress Cataloging-in-Publication Data [to come]

Names: Munro, Karen, 1973- author.
Title: Tactical urbanism for librarians : quick, low-cost ways to make big
    changes / Karen Munro.
Description: Chicago : ALA Editions, an imprint of the American Library
    Association, 2017. | Includes bibliographical references and index.
Identifiers: LCCN 2017007493| ISBN 9780838915585 (pbk. : alk. paper) | ISBN
    9780838915844 (PDF) | ISBN 9780838915851 (ePub) | ISBN 9780838915868
    (Kindle)
Subjects: LCSH: Library planning. | Libraries and community. | Libraries and
    metropolitan areas. | Libraries—Sociological aspects. | Libraries—Case
    studies. | Organizational change. | City planning—Citizen participation.
    | Urban renewal—United States—Citizen participation—Case studies.
Classification: LCC Z678 .M96 2017 | DDC 025.1—dc23 LC record available at https://
lccn.loc.gov/2017007493

Book design by Kimberly Thornton in the Questa, Korolev Military Stencil, and Intro Rust typefaces. Cover image © Lwzfoto/Adobe Stock.

♾ This paper meets the requirements of ANSI/NISO Z39.48–1992 (Permanence of Paper).

Printed in the United States of America
21 20 19 18 17   5 4 3 2 1

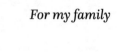

For my family

CONTENTS

ACKNOWLEDGMENTS

MY SINCERE THANKS TO ALL THE LIBRARIANS WHO SPOKE WITH ME ABOUT THE projects in this book, to the resource-sharing and interlibrary loan librarians and library staff who helped me amass the vast number of books and articles that I read as background, to everyone who published their work so I could find out about it in the first place, and to everyone who keeps trying out cheap, quick, creative ways to make libraries work better for everyone.

AN INTRODUCTION TO
TACTICAL URBANISM

Once Upon a Time in DUMBO . . .

N SPRING 2007, A TRUCK PULLED UP TO A SMALL, GARBAGE-strewn parking lot under the Manhattan Bridge in Brooklyn. The lot was described by people who knew it as "forlorn" and "barren" (Chan 2007; Naparstek 2007). It had space for about a dozen cars on an ungainly triangle of land where Pearl Street and Anchorage Place meet, just a few blocks south of the East River. New York is full of these oddly shaped bits of wasteland, many of them created when long avenues were overlaid on the existing street grid. In this one, Anchorage Place follows the diagonal path of the Manhattan Bridge Lower Roadway and its overpass, which looms over the lot on its west side. It was a valuable little piece of the DUMBO neighborhood in Brooklyn, but it wasn't a pretty spot, or one where most people would want to linger.

The truck was from the New York City Department of Transportation. It carried a load of green paint, and its crew had specific instructions about how to apply it. They unloaded their gear and started to work.

By August the cars were long gone. The concrete triangle of the lot was painted bright grassy green, shade umbrellas and public seating had been installed, and planters overflowed with trees and flowers. In lieu of a raised curb, a double white line separated the new "pocket park" from the streets around it, with enormous granite blocks acting as bollards. Local artists had brought sculpture and distinctive handmade furniture. A local food truck began visiting the park during weekday lunch hours. The former parking lot even got a new name—the Pearl Street Triangle.

And the work didn't end there. In March 2010, the neighborhood held an Ideas Competition to improve the park even more (dumbonyc 2010). Eight proposals suggested everything from adding another subway stop for the elevated line that runs above the park to creating tiered amphitheater seating for public performances to transforming the triangle-shaped park into an enormous interactive piano keyboard. Thanks to an arts grant, in 2012 the green paint was replaced with an enormous mural by artist David Ellis, depicting a pair of giant hands supporting a brightly colored body. In 2016, a weekly farmer's market moved in, bringing everything from fresh produce and eggs to "old-fashioned-style barrel pickles" (Frishberg 2016).

What started with a few buckets of green paint and a few extra granite blocks from the Washington Bridge has become an "urban oasis" and "the heart of the DUMBO community" (DUMBO Improvement District 2012, 2015). Happily, the park seems to prove the truth of the Hollywood cliché: if you build it, they will come.

But there's more to the story.

The success of the Pearl Street Triangle, and dozens of other "pocket parks" like it throughout New York City, owes as much to careful planning, solid partnerships, and visionary leadership as it does to grassroots, can-do creative spirit. It owes a great deal to the big-picture strategies of the New York City Department of Transportation and to Mayor Michael Bloomberg's PlaNYC program, which aims to create more open public spaces throughout the city (Chan 2007). It owes much to the DUMBO neighborhood's Business Improvement District, which brokered deals with local artists and restaurants to make the park lively and distinctive. But it owes perhaps the most to the controversial work style of New York City's transportation commissioner from 2007 to 2013, Janette Sadik-Khan.

It was during Sadik-Khan's term that the Pearl Street Triangle was realized—not just conceived, described, or approved, but cleaned up, painted, planted, and furnished. It was during her term that more than sixty pub-lic parks and plazas were created across the city, most in spaces that were considered ungainly, inefficient, or useless (Sadik-Khan 2016). And although Sadik-Khan made a lot of nice places for New Yorkers to sit, she's perhaps even better known for getting them onto their bikes.

During her seven years with the Department of Transportation, Sadik-Khan claims that the city added almost four hundred miles of bike lanes (Lindsey 2015). During the same period, surveys show that bicycle com-muting rose from just under twenty thousand to over thirty-six thousand cyclists (Flegenheimer 2013). In 2007 the New York City Department of Transportation's twelve-hour Midtown Bicycle Count, which counts bicy-clists passing predetermined points throughout the city on a given day between 7 a.m. and 7 p.m., averaged 13,205 trips per year (New York City Department of Transportation 2015). By 2013 that same twelve-hour count had leaped to over twenty-one thousand trips. Broadway Avenue, one of the world's most famous and iconic streets, closed half its lanes to car traffic to make room for a bike path and a pedestrian zone (Neuman 2008). Times Square, the garish neon heart of the city, was closed to traffic com-pletely and became a pedestrian haven.

How did Sadik-Khan do it? How did she change one of America's densest, most car-congested cities into a place riddled with bike lanes and neighborhood parks? How did she overcome the New York City atti-tudes, temperaments, and belief systems—not to mention the entrenched agency officials and taxi unions—that make a two-wheeled, park-loving revolution seem not just unlikely but almost impossible?

And what does all this have to do with libraries?

This book aims to explore the answer to all these questions through the frame of something called *tactical urbanism*. You may have heard of tac-tical urbanism before, although maybe not in the context of the New York City transportation commissioner. Instead, you may have heard of knit bombing, guerrilla gardening, depaving, pop-up shops, or programs like Play Streets and PARK(ing) Day. Maybe you've even participated in some form of tactical urbanism yourself, painting a mural on an intersection in your neighborhood or closing down your street for a summertime block party (with or without a permit, ahem).

Or maybe none of this is familiar to you, and the phrase *tactical urbanism* sounds like the next retail trend, inspired by The Hunger Games. So before we go any farther, let's break open that phrase and start examining what a DUMBO pocket park has to do with your library.

What Is Tactical Urbanism? (And Why Should Librarians Care?)

Tactical urbanism is a relatively recent coinage to describe a type of action that people have been taking for centuries. The phrase itself isn't written in stone—you might see terms as various as guerrilla urbanism, city repair, DIY urbanism, hands-on urbanism, participatory urbanism, and pop-up urbanism used to describe the same ideas. The nonprofit Project for Public Spaces has coined its own term—Lighter, Quicker, Cheaper—which at least helps isolate three of the central concepts in play.

But apart from those three words, what do all these phrases actually mean? Most loosely, tactical urbanism can be defined as any action designed to improve a city or neighborhood with minimal oversight, budget, and delay. Tactical urbanism is local, it's hands-on, it's immediate, and it can usually be accomplished without a lot of training or resources. Author Kim A. O'Connell describes it this way: "Tactical urbanism refers to temporary, cheap, and usually grassroots interventions—including so-called guerrilla gardens, pop-up parks, food carts, and 'open streets' projects—that are designed to improve city life on a block-by-block, street-by-street basis" (2013).

Of course, concepts such as "cheap," "grassroots," and even "local" are relative and open to interpretation. Although it costs almost nothing to walk or bike around your neighborhood scattering wildflower seeds into abandoned lots, it might cost upward of $5,000 to install a "parkmobile" consisting of a custom dumpster planted with tree ferns and yucca plants. Although you can knit a cozy jacket around a bike rack in your neighborhood all by yourself, you might need a planning committee and some lead time to pry up the concrete in a vacant lot and plant a community food garden. And although your neighborhood community group might creatively lobby for a new crosswalk by painting a temporary one where it's needed, it takes a lot more political clout to install four hundred miles of bike lanes in New York City. And yet all these projects participate in the spirit of tactical urbanism to different degrees and in different ways.

At its most basic, tactical urbanism is something that just about anyone can do. There's really no such thing as a "professional" or "expert" tactical urbanist, so it's no surprise that different practitioners describe the concept differently. Working in a largely American context, urban designer and planner Mike Lydon and his colleagues define tactical urbanism as sharing the following characteristics:

- A deliberate, phased approach to instigating change;
- The offering of local solutions for local planning challenges;
- Short-term commitment and realistic expectations;
- Low-risks, with a possibly high reward; and
- The development of social capital between citizens and the building of organizational capacity between public-private institutions, non-profits, and their constituents. (2015, 1–2)

Museum of Modern Art curator Barry Bergdoll, writing about tactical urbanism in the context of the developing world, describes it a little more radically:

Tactical urbanism . . . is a highly pragmatic movement that abandons all holistic and comprehensive planning as either failed in its historical record or doomed by the worldwide ascent of neo-liberal economy and politics. It is, however, an elastic movement in that it applies to a spectrum of designers, from those who perform guerrilla intervention for short-term change . . . to those who seek to prod, provoke, or stimulate the political process toward incremental realization of fragments of what might be larger networks. (Gadanho 2014, 12)

Besides the ones that O'Connell, Lydon and colleagues, and Bergdoll point out, tactical urbanist projects also tend to demonstrate some of the following characteristics: a reliance on ingenuity, a preference for rapid deployment, a willingness to experiment and revise in process, a tolerance for error and perceived failure, an ability to value intangible benefits such as new and improved relationships and proof of concept, and a willingness to start (and sometimes stay) small.

Cheap, grassroots, temporary, ingenious, adroit, experimental, pragmatic, deliberate, local, short-term, realistic, low-risk, elastic, provocative—taken together, these qualities start to cohere into a clearer profile. Tactical urbanism is scrappy, persistent, and creative. It makes the best possible use of limited resources and looks for hands-on ways to solve immediate problems (no crosswalk, ugly vacant lots) in service to a larger strategy (improving and beautifying the city). There's still more to it, too, as we'll see throughout this book. Tactical urbanism, because it's performed largely by ordinary people in service to other ordinary people, is inherently human, humane, optimistic . . . and often whimsical, creative, delightful, charming, and funny. These qualities tend to arise naturally from the act of doing things in a tactical, human-centered way. They're also practically useful and worth cultivating, because they engage and sustain people and offer an alternate means of remuneration. Warm fuzzies can't take the place of cold, hard salary, but they can motivate people to do amazing things.

Wait . . . What Are Tactics Again?

It's pretty important to point out at the start that tactical urbanism takes its name from tactics rather than from strategy. Tactics, whether they're military, political, or part of a chess game, are inherently tied to strategy without being synonymous with it. A strategy is a big-picture plan designed to achieve a major long-term goal. Strategies imply the outlay of sizable resources—money, time, and people—as well as the considered, official imprimatur of an organization or institution.

Tactics, on the other hand, happen at a smaller scale. Organizationally speaking, tactics are the tasks and actions that will move you toward your strategic goals. If strategy answers the question "Why are we doing this?," then tactics answer the question "How are we getting it done?" Tactics are immediate, practical, and limited in scope. They happen at the grassroots, local level. They're quick to mount and often quick to disappear.

So why are tactics worth thinking about? After all, we don't create professional aspirations around the day-to-day. We create them around long-term goals and directions—around strategy. Why spend time thinking about short-term, low-risk projects when what we really want is to build a city—or a library—that will thrive and flourish a decade or a century from now?

As Mike Lydon and his colleagues remind us, "If done well, these small scale changes are conceived as the first step in realizing lasting change. Thus, tactical urbanism is most effective when used in conjunction with long term planning efforts" (2015, 2). Operating from a tactical mind-set doesn't mean acting randomly or without consideration (more on that later in this chapter). In an ideal world, tactics and strategy work hand in hand—tactics help deliver what strategies dream up. In a less-than-ideal world, where strategy can get bogged down, abstract, or disconnected from reality, a tactical intervention can be a way to reboot the strategic planning process in new relationship to concrete, real-world factors. Curator and architect Pedro Gadanho describes tactical urbanism as "acupunctural interventions" (2014, 19). Like the single, tiny needles of acupuncture, tactical interventions can be powerful points of action, radiating energy to create a larger network of change.

Okay, but Really—What Does This Have to Do with Libraries?

A lot. At least, I think so. This book works from the premises that cities and libraries have a lot in common and that librarians can learn from tactical urbanist projects of all different types and scales. Here's why.

Librarians who want to change libraries face many of the same challenges faced by ordinary citizens, city planners, and even lofty transportation commissioners who want to change cities. Many of us have to do things we're not trained, equipped, or funded to do. Sometimes we have to fix or create things we're not even clearly charged with fixing or creating, simply because they so obviously need to happen. (Check out Terry Reese's [2013a] MarcEdit project, for instance.) Many of us operate from a position of daily intimacy with the issue at hand. We walk on the broken sidewalk, or use the flawed software, or dream of the renovated exhibition space every day. Many of us have to create our action plan on the fly, developing our ideas, narrative, and partnerships as we go. We're not experts. We're thoughtful, energetic, creative, occasionally slightly obsessed people with ideas. Tactics offer us all a framework for action that's flexible, extensible, and fun to use—and that has proven to be effective whether you're flush with cash or broke.

Because tactical urbanism is defined by a creative, resilient, democratic response to challenges, and because it typically operates in service to a larger purpose (a better neighborhood, a better library), it's a potent complement to traditional organizational structures. In other words, your library can probably encourage a tactical culture without conflicting with existing hierarchies, reporting structures, budgets, and so on. In fact, I'll hope to show that a tactics-friendly mentality is a healthy component of any library's culture. We'll talk more about that in the section of this book that directly addresses library administrators.

If you're still feeling dubious about whether a knit-bombing, depaving, guerrilla-gardening ethos has any place in libraries, remember that though libraries today might have a reputation for staid traditionalism and bureaucracy, they also have a historical entanglement with social upheaval. As Scott McLemee (2011) wrote in an *Inside Higher Ed* article about the Occupy Wall Street library in Zuccotti Park, "Libraries emerged as part of the sit-down strikes that unionized the American auto industry in the 1930s" as well as in worker-run education centers for low-income users established around the country. Librarians have been at the forefront of civil protest and activism against government policies of surveillance, invasion of privacy, and censorship—even when that protest was at its most costly, such as in the aftermath of the September 11 attacks in the United States or in modern-day Mali, where Al Qaeda has attempted to confiscate and destroy historic Islamic books and manuscripts. Throughout history, libraries have been sites of social engagement, subversion, innovation, and even revolution. At times, the very business of conserving, preserving, and providing access has been a radical affair. As we weigh the importance of some of our institutional habits and traditions, we must remember that just as librarians have at times been conservative, risk-averse, and conventional, we have also been progressive, open-minded, and even revolutionary.

So Are We Talking about Cities or Libraries?

That's a good question. Let's consider the modern city—a large (sometimes vast) and complicated organization with a lengthy personal history. A city is traditional, retentive, and conservative by nature. It represents vast sums of public investment as well as vast areas of public liability. It's shared by people from all walks of life, all income levels, all religions and ethnicities. It's run by a bureaucracy, usually made up of experts. Its operations are rife with loopholes, exceptions, requirements, regulations, standard practices, omissions, and work-arounds. It's hierarchical, yet its membership and leadership change over time. A city has institutional memory, although occasionally that memory's faulty. A city needs money and is perpetually short of it. It has a public image to uphold. It exists because of, and for, people—but sometimes that fact gets forgotten in the complex, challenging, occasionally tedious business of making the place run.

If you're a librarian, some or all of this might sound familiar. Libraries and cities have a lot in common, and that means that librarians have a lot in common with the people who run cities. And that includes not just elected officials and civil servants but ordinary citizens. We all participate in the life of cities, just as all library users participate in the life of the library. Libraries, like cities, are first and foremost about people. That's an underlying principle of tactical urbanism—that everyone who lives in the city has the right to speak up about issues and conditions and to participate in changing or solving them. If we transfer the idea to libraries, then we should assume that we all—librarians, administrators, staff, and patrons—have the same right and obligation to act within and upon our organization.

It's worth noting that as we'll see throughout this book, the Venn diagram of tactical interventions in libraries and cities shares a lot of middle ground. The L!brary Initiative in New York City is a citywide attempt to address poverty and improve childhood education through improving elementary and middle school libraries. The cities of Magdeburg, Germany, and Newmarket, Canada, created innovative library buildings to boost their economies and social cohesion. In Texas and Missouri, towns with abandoned big-box stores reenergized their streets by creating libraries in those unused spaces. In Cleveland, the public library's outdoor summertime art installations benefit a whole neighborhood.

Libraries are essentially communal organizations, so it's no surprise that many of the case studies we'll explore have implications not only for the libraries themselves but for the towns and cities in which they're situated. It's also no surprise that the essentially democratic, humanist values of tactical urbanism translate so well into the library context.

Okay, but My Library Won't Go for It

You might work in a library that dearly needs some creative, innovative, tactical interventions—and yet your library leaders might not want to hear a single word about "tactical anything." Or you yourself might be a library administrator who's overburdened, underfunded, or otherwise unable to add any new ideas to your plate. Or maybe you think things are going just fine at your library—and maybe you're right. Maybe your library is already a nimble organization that gives its staff and members full rein to creatively and cost-effectively test ideas that serve its larger goals while responding quickly to fix problems as they arise and supporting trials of new projects that push your library into new, exciting territory. (Hooray for you!)

But if that's not the case and your library is likely or certain to resist "tactical anything," I hope this book will give you some fuel to keep the conversation going. I hope the urbanist and library case studies here will inspire you with their adroit, thoughtful, persistent, and ingenious responses to a variety of types of problems, including bureaucratic intransigence. (You're not alone!) In the spirit of tactical agility, I hope that if your library isn't ready for a tactical approach to administration or advocacy, maybe you can still get traction on a tactical approach to space design or streamlining your integrated library system (ILS) or something else entirely.

As you explore your options, remember that your approach matters. After we dive deeper into our case studies, we'll discuss how a tactical, DIY, or "guerrilla" approach can still be professional, positive, and collaborative. That might sound counterintuitive, but just as there's no such thing as an "expert" tactical urbanist, there's no hard-and-fast rule about how tacticians can or should work with existing organizational structures. Certainly many tactical interventionists take the role of gadfly, provoking those in authority into action. Others operate around the fringes of the mainstream power structure, creating playful or creative interventions without a strong political bent. And some tacticians (like Janette Sadik-Khan) are already in positions of organizational power and influence, affording them unique opportunities to introduce a tactical approach at a higher level.

Whether tacticians seek to collaborate with managers and gatekeepers or spur them into action, tone and approach are vital. Although Sadik-Khan unquestionably accomplished a huge amount as transportation commissioner, she also garnered criticism, both within the city administration and outside it. Her preference for moving fast, cutting red tape, and fostering disruptive change gained her a reputation for being "dismissive and confrontational," among other things (Grynbaum 2011). In an organizational setting, alienating colleagues and partners can spell doom for the best, most creative ideas for change.

Shannon Mattern, writing in *Places* magazine, puts it well. Even while praising the benefits of a particularly relevant form of tactical urbanism—Little Free Libraries—she acknowledges that "we can't allow our propensity to romanticize the nimble and provisional, and to admire the ingenuity of 'pop up' culture, to blind us to the fact that operating a library is a logistically complicated endeavor that requires significant infrastructure and professional expertise—and public support" (2012). Strategy without tactics is static and irrelevant. But tactics without strategy are rootless, inconsistent, and ephemeral. We need both to get ahead.

Okay, but They Really Won't Go for It

If you want to bring resistant colleagues or administrators on board with a tactical approach to a project, it might be helpful to try to anticipate some of the reasons why they might reject "tactical anything." Because tactical urbanism is our model, let's start there. We've seen that it can be hard to pin down exactly what tactical urbanism is, so let's take a minute to say what it isn't.

It's Not Chaos

Tactical urbanism isn't just "everyone doing their own thing." Some of the projects we've already mentioned—tossing seed bombs into vacant lots, for instance—are pretty unregulated, it's true. But we've also mentioned that a tactical approach is by definition tied to a larger goal or strategy. Although most tactical urbanist interventions are grassroots in comparison to official City Hall bureaucratic structure, they are strategically tied to the needs of the community. In the case of seed-bombing in a vacant lot, the larger strategy is to activate an urban asset (space) left fallow by the official power structure. When Janette Sadik-Khan commandeered that garbage-strewn DUMBO parking lot to turn it into a city park, she was furthering Mayor Bloomberg's PlaNYC strategy, which seeks to improve New Yorkers' access to parks and open spaces.

It's Not Revolt

If tactical urbanism is a revolution, it's a gentle one. Although tactical urbanists do seek to change the status quo, and some of their methods may skirt the fringes of legality, tactical urbanism shouldn't conjure images of troops taking to the streets. Some forms of tactical urbanism do overlap with civil disobedience, it's true—the open-air libraries of the Occupy Wall Street movement come immediately to mind, as do some street-reclaiming projects such as DIY crosswalks and PARK(ing) Day. But as an approach to change-making, tactical urbanism is collaborative, participatory, and open to working with existing power structures (often playfully and creatively) rather than demolishing them.

It's Not Change for Its Own Sake

Tactical urbanism isn't a matter of doing something just because you can. All too many librarians are familiar with the concept of "death by a thousand projects." Libraries have many different audiences and constituencies whom they are asked to serve in many different ways. Academic libraries might be tasked with records management or instructional technology support on their campuses. Public libraries may offer free lunch programs for low-income kids and community workshops on job searching and professional retooling. And everyone's installing a maker space. Some of these projects are things we're excited to work on, while others may be mandated by circumstance. A tactical approach to libraries wouldn't support leaping into every new opportunity that comes along just because it's there. Instead, the tactical librarian should look for quick, low-cost, low-threshold ways to do work that serves the organization's larger strategies.

It's Not a Sweeping Reversal of the Institution's Goals or Direction

Perhaps because tactical urbanism is known by many other names, including *guerrilla*, *grassroots*, and *DYI urbanism*, it can carry a certain revolutionary whiff. But in fact most tactical urbanism is small-scale and incremental. Because most projects are low- or no-budget and can be accomplished by ordinary people, they don't radically upend the status quo. Even a powerhouse like Janette Sadik-Khan started out relatively small, with a few public parks and plazas—and importantly, she built on the good work already begun by other officials and agencies. Tactical urbanism aims not only to accomplish a short-term tactical goal but also to engage creatively with the official power structure. The idea isn't just to depave that vacant lot but to show how things could be better, get people interested and engaged, and use that imaginative and social capital to spur the city works department to build a playground there instead.

Okay . . . I'm Interested. Now What?

Great! This book is for you! Let's quickly preview what we'll cover next.

We'll look first at some case studies of tactical urbanism to flesh out the definitions we've been using here. After all, tactical urbanism spans a broad continuum including everything from engaging in civil protest to finding creative ways to cut cost, process, and time from within the system itself. Concrete examples will help us get a handle on what is otherwise a big, boisterous, slightly messy category of ideas and actions.

Then we'll spend a little time distilling some key characteristics from the case studies. Apart from "light, quick, and cheap," what elements define a tactical approach to any project or problem? We'll try to put names to some of the more ineffable qualities that we see over and over in successful tactical urbanist projects so that we can look for them in library contexts as well.

We'll then dive into the world of library tactics. Because this book is intended to be useful and interesting for all types of librarians, we'll look at examples of tactical interventions in many different areas of library work, from building successful advocacy campaigns to hacking the ILS to building and renovating new library spaces. It might surprise you to see how the principles of tactical work can translate into some of these settings—or, after you spend some time considering the creativity, ingenuity, and flexibility inherent to tactical urbanist projects, it might not.

Because libraries and cities are often so closely interconnected, we'll use a separate section to examine some tactical interventions that straddle the city–library line. Communities campaigning for neighborhood branch libraries, libraries staging public art exhibitions, and open-air libraries bringing people together to read their own books—these are some of the creative, rule-bending case studies we'll consider.

From there, we'll take a step back and consider some of the broader contexts in which you might undertake a tactical project. What conditions might lead you to try new tactics—a problem, a need for change, or just a desire to grow? How, in each situation, might you modify your approach? What downsides are there to using tactics, and what's reasonable to expect from your intervention?

Maybe you're reading all this with interest and thinking, this all sounds great, but I'm a library director. I'm in charge of big-picture, long-term strategic planning. Tactics seem to be about short-term, low-cost ways to work around organizational hierarchy and bureaucracy. They're about working laterally, with decentralized user communities and grassroots methods. Where do I fit in? That's a great question, so we'll spend a little time talking about how library administrators can help create—and benefit from—a tactics-friendly environment in the library.

We'll finish with a list of twelve ways you can make your library projects more tactical. These aren't specific, paint-by-numbers instructions for what to do in any given situation. Instead, they're reminders of the attitudes and approaches you can cultivate to accomplish things quickly, cheaply, and effectively in your library. No two libraries are the same. No two librarians are, either. You'll have to decide for yourself exactly how, when, and why to take a tactical approach in your workplace. I hope this book will inspire you to reassess the value of experimentation, creativity, communication, collaboration, and delight in your work—and to seize opportunities to create them whenever you can.

2

TACTICAL URBANISM
CASE STUDIES

TO GROUND OUR DISCUSSION OF A TACTICAL APPROACH TO library work, we'll start by looking at some examples of tactical urbanism projects, or *interventions*, as they're sometimes called. (Tactical urbanists are said to be "intervening" in a situation on behalf of their community or another interested party.) In each case we'll describe the intervention, then explore the conditions that led to it and draw out some of the principles that helped it succeed. In the next section, we'll look at how those same conditions and principles apply in tactical library projects.

TACTICAL URBANISM CASE STUDY 1:
THE ASTORIA SCUM RIVER BRIDGE

In the Astoria neighborhood of Queens, New York, a leaking pipe had been creating a public nuisance on the sidewalk beneath Amtrak's Hell Gate Bridge Viaduct approach for more than twenty years. Dirty water puddled in summer and formed an icy slick in winter. The spot was on a well-trafficked sidewalk near a subway stop, and the problem was so well known that local residents dubbed it the "Astoria Scum River."

In 2009, local artists Posterchild and Jason Eppink used salvaged wood from a discarded bench to build a small footbridge that spanned the puddle. They stationed it on the sidewalk, complete with a cheeky metal plaque christening it the "Astoria Scum River Bridge" and dedicating it to "the safety and comfort of the pedestrian." Pedestrians started using the bridge immediately—and not just using it, but photographing it, blogging about it, Tweeting, Facebooking, and as a result notifying local media.

Within weeks, Eppink and Posterchild were contacted by Jonathan Szott, who then served as constituent liaison for New York City Council member Peter Vallone. Szott's e-mail thanked the artists for creating the bridge and informed them that "our office had a meeting with Amtrak and discussed some solutions beginning with cleaning out the existing drop inlets that are filled with debris. A time line for alleviating the problem will be developed shortly" (Eppink 2010). In fact, thanks in part to the media splash, Amtrak sent workers to fix the problem within days (Bennett 2010).

A month later Eppink and Posterchild retired the bridge because the sidewalk was clean and dry. The salvaged wood went back to the curb, and the Astoria Scum River was no more.

Key Principles: Why It Matters to Libraries

Conditions and Causes

The Astoria Scum River problem existed for decades. It was a known neighborhood nuisance that had faded into near-invisibility because the borough and Amtrak had ignored the problem for so long. The people most affected by it—neighborhood residents—didn't have the skills or administrative permission to fix it themselves, and past complaints had gone unheeded by the people who did have those things. Most residents were only affected by the problem occasionally, maybe a few times a day as they traveled around the neighborhood. Because this was a community problem, it ended up being "nobody's problem," and even people who were angry or frustrated about the situation could more easily put up with it as an intermittent nuisance than they could figure out how to fix it.

There are invisible, entrenched problems in most organizations, and libraries are no exception. Invisible problems are probably the most common type of problem that we face. At times we might not even know we're facing them—they're so small that they go unnoticed. Maybe nobody knows that you can flip up the current periodicals shelves to find the recent back issues. (Does anyone ever figure that out on their own?) Maybe you have a web guide that you've been meaning to update for ages because the image is stretched and wonky—but the content is good, and who can find the time?

Every day we all experience (or ignore) a hundred little moments where things could be better. They aren't enough to derail us completely, so most of us address problems like these by tolerating them unless they reach some kind of crisis point that forces us to fix them. In his 2015 TED talk "The first secret of design is . . . noticing," inventor and senior Apple executive Tony Fadell considers the example of the sticker that comes on a piece of fruit—unpleasant to peel off and hard to dispose of because it's so sticky. But how many of us would consider it an actual "problem" worthy of a solution? Instead we just live with it. Fadell suggests that this is because we become psychologically habituated to minor, chronic annoyances. We can't notice everything all the time, so it's more comfortable just to endure the annoyance and move on.

But like Eppink and Posterchild, Fadell has a history of fixing invisible problems. Years ago at Apple, he noticed the annoying requirement for customers to charge their brand-new laptops for several hours before using them. Instead of ignoring that irritant, Fadell convinced Apple to charge new devices longer in the warehouse, so that they would arrive in customers' hands ready to go right away. A minor change, but customers loved it, and it set a new standard for the industry. Today almost no electronic devices from any major manufacturer need charging when you unbox them.

Fadell has some advice for noticing invisible problems: look broader, look closer, and think younger. By "look broader," he means look at the conditions on either side of a problem you're considering. What conditions create it, and what conditions does it create? How do they contribute to the problem? Can they be changed or removed? By "look closer," he means to pay close attention to details. Sometimes significant problems are embedded in the tiniest aspects of our lives and habits. By "think younger," he means to strive for the open perspective of a child, a stranger, or a beginner.

Fadell's advice may ring true for you if you (like most of us) encounter lots of little library problems that don't seem worth the effort of fixing. Thinking broadly about how those problems affect your users and your staff (and you) might help motivate you to address them. Thinking closely about the specific intervention that will fix the problem might take some time, but it might also pay big dividends. And thinking young, without preconceptions about the problem or its solution, might open up whole new avenues of creativity, wit, and delight.

The Nature of the Intervention

Eppink and Posterchild created *a local solution for a local challenge*. Rather than lobby their council member or the company for a solution (which would require understanding the bureaucracy enough to know whom to contact), they asked themselves what skills they had to fix the problem. They knew enough basic carpentry to build a bridge over the puddle, and that was enough to get the ball rolling.

They approached the problem with *creativity and ingenuity*. You could say that the problem was the leaky pipes. But Eppink and Posterchild didn't have the skills, money, or permission to drill out and replace the pipes, or the political capital to convince elected officials or business leaders to do the job. Instead of lapsing into apathy or frustration, they creatively reconceived the problem. If they couldn't fix the pipes, they could fix the puddle itself by building a temporary bridge across it.

They built *social capital* with their neighbors without even seeing them. Although Eppink and Posterchild worked alone to build and install the bridge, the fact that they created a tangible, visible artifact was an implicit response to the needs of the neighborhood and an invitation for others to engage with the problem. They also added the cheeky dedication plaque, using *humor* and self-deprecation to build goodwill among pedestrians. The bridge wasn't just utilitarian—it had charm, and it offered an element of *delight*. Without ever directly asking for people to spread the word, Eppink and Posterchild effectively enlisted a small army of allies to document the project and encourage (or shame) the official power structure into paying attention.

Eppink and Posterchild's project epitomizes a *short-term, low-risk commitment*. Building the bridge from scrap material cost next to nothing except the artists' time and energy. If it didn't draw local attention or force a bigger change, at least it would still get people safely across the puddle. When it did succeed in getting the pipes repaired, Eppink and Posterchild retired the bridge. You could say that the bridge was a failure because it was returned to the trash heap so soon after it was built. But the bridge was never really the goal—instead, it was a tool to engage the official power structure in implementing a better solution.

TACTICAL URBANISM CASE STUDY 2: GUERRILLA GARDENING

GUERRILLA GARDENING IS MOST BROADLY DEFINED AS CULTIVATING LAND TO which you have no formal legal claim, often with the express intent of making a political statement or changing land policy. That's a pretty broad definition, and indeed, the full scope of guerrilla gardening could encompass everything from disputes between indigenous peoples and land developers to suburban neighborhoods with restrictive homeowners' agreements. Some people even count Johnny Appleseed as one of the original guerrilla gardeners, scattering his orchards. Unlike the Astoria Scum River Bridge, there's no single instance to point to as the essence or even the origin of the action.

To narrow it down, let's consider one particularly famous and well-documented example of guerrilla gardening. In the early 1970s, Brooklyn resident Liz Christy began working with friends and neighbors who shared her frustration with urban decay in the borough. Calling themselves the Green Guerrillas, they planted rogue flower beds in parking strips and tossed what they termed "seed green-aids" (balls of clay and seeds) into vacant lots (Green Guerrillas, n.d.).

Over time the Green Guerrillas came to focus their efforts on a vacant plot of city-owned land at Houston Street and Bowery. Denny Lee wrote in the *New York Times*, "In 1973, the group took over the site, which was then strewn with rubble, laid down topsoil and began planting. The following year, the city agreed to rent the space to the gardeners for $1 a month, and the city's first community garden was created" (2001).

The rest is history. As of 2016, New York City had more than five hundred community gardens and more than three hundred school gardens, offering residents space to grow food, flowers, and more. The city's GreenThumb program provides assistance and oversight for gardeners and even publishes information on how to start a new community garden (New York City Department of Parks and Recreation, n.d.). In 1985, the original site at Bowery and Houston was renamed the Liz Christy Community Garden, and the Green Guerrillas organization continues to nurture gardens in New York City to this day.

Key Principles: Why It Matters to Libraries

Conditions and Causes

In the 1970s, New York City wasn't the city it is today. Manhattan wasn't synonymous with astronomical real estate prices, world-class tourism destinations, and amenities for the uber-rich. Instead, the city was teetering on the verge of bankruptcy and was a punch line for jokes (and fears) about blight, crime, and poverty. New York wasn't alone—many other major American cities experienced "white flight," economic decline, and inner-city decay from the 1950s through the 1980s. But the problems were so large-scale, stemming from macro-level economic, demographic, and urbanization trends, that they seemed insurmountable. Even President Ford initially declined to bail New York City out of its debt crisis—a decision for which he was publicly lambasted and which he eventually reversed.

The problems in 1970s New York City weren't invisible, like the Astoria Scum River or the sticker that comes on your supermarket apple. They were big, hairy, and scary. They were the kinds of problems we might call both complex and complicated. Those terms might seem redundant, but in fact they mean different things to mathematicians, psychologists, sociologists, and others who study problems for a living.

The classic example of a complicated problem is the moon shot—putting a live human being on the moon and getting him or her safely back. The logistics involved in a moon landing are incredible. The job requires experts from many different fields to work together in pursuit of a single goal. It takes specialized knowledge and training, coordination, communication, and integration. But in the end, what needs to be accomplished is knowable—everyone understands the goal, and there are protocols, time lines, and agreed-upon measures of success.

A complex problem is different. Instead of putting someone on the moon, imagine that your job is to raise a child. The official definition of a complex problem is one that isn't just complicated (or stressful) but that has no clearly defined "right" way to do things, no established protocol for its solution, and no guarantee of success even if you have prior experience solving the same or similar problems. Complex problems, unlike simple or even complicated ones, don't behave the same way every time. They're nonlinear, dynamic, adaptive, and uncertain. In other words, you don't always know what stage you're in when you're trying to fix a complex problem. Complex problems change in response to their environments and even their own component elements, making them deeply unpredictable. You can't just take a complex problem or situation apart to understand how it works. Like children, complex problems are both unique and a little bit chaotic.

The problems facing major American cities in the 1970s weren't just complicated, requiring many experts and agencies to work together to fix a known issue or accomplish a goal. They were also complex, meaning that unpredictable elements like social changes, economic fluctuations, and demographic movements played a role. All of this might sound familiar to modern librarians, who are faced with huge, disruptive social changes like the Internet, mobile technologies, shrinking budgets, changes to higher education and community service models, changing attitudes, and more. Like the Green Guerrillas, librarians must live with the products and consequences of vast systemic movements far beyond our control. Complicated and complex problems affect us daily, and we must decide how to respond.

The Nature of the Intervention

Faced with a city on the verge of collapse, Christy and the Green Guerrillas didn't let themselves get overwhelmed. Instead they focused on a small part of the whole and created a *concrete, achievable goal*. They didn't try to fix the whole city or even a neighborhood. They paid attention to what was right in front of them—first parking strips and medians and then a single vacant lot that had potential. They started small and grew larger over time, using a *deliberate phased approach* to create what would eventually become a worldwide movement.

Like most ordinary people, the Green Guerrillas had limited resources. They didn't have enough money to buy all the materials they'd need to create their first garden, so they found a *partner*. The Green Guerrillas contributed the labor necessary to clear rubble from the lot and start planting, while the city donated the land and the soil. From the city's point of view the partnership was *low-risk* because the land was already unused and the cost of the soil was minimal. If the experiment failed, the neighborhood couldn't be worse off than when it started, but if it succeeded, then there would be a glimmer of hope for others.

The Green Guerrillas *scaled up their project* to make a strategic impression. Sunflowers in parking strips are fun, but they don't convey permanence, investment, or the ability to make change at a larger scale. If the Guerrillas had kept working at that level, they wouldn't have attracted the city's trust and investment. If they'd tried to leap from sunflowers to a Bureau of Community Gardens, for instance, they would have been seen as naive and unqualified. Instead they staged the project thoughtfully to offer realistic, valuable rewards for everyone, asking for minimal investment from the city and residents.

Central to the Green Guerrillas' work is the vision, energy, and optimism that it took to look at a lot full of rubble and trash and see a garden. Remember, New York City was a very different place. Today a vacant lot in

New York looks to most people like a gold mine. In 1973 there was no guarantee that the city would dig itself out of its financial and social woes. The Guerrillas needed to be able to blinker themselves to the overwhelming messages of their times—the garbage fires, the movies like Escape from New York positing Manhattan as a dystopic prison island, the racial and social unrest—and commit themselves to generating generous, humane, and positive outcomes for the city. Intangible assets might be hard to quantify, but they're essential to any tactical intervention.

TACTICAL URBANISM CASE STUDY 3: PARK(ING) DAY

SOME TACTICAL URBANIST PROJECTS AREN'T MEANT TO LAST. PARK(ING) DAY IS a little different from the other case studies we've looked at, because it's intentionally ephemeral, leaving no lasting footprint—not even for a few weeks, like Eppink and Posterchild's bridge. In fact, you might consider it not so much an urban intervention as a work of art, an event, or simply the ultimate proof of concept.

On the third Friday in September, in cities around the world, people start plugging parking meters with coins and cards. But they don't park their cars in the spots—instead, they set up Astroturf and picnic tables, umbrellas and benches. They bring musical instruments, food, bocce balls, and Frisbees. They unfold Ping Pong and Foosball tables. Then they settle in to enjoy the space along the curb where cars would otherwise sit, until their time on the meter is up. In other words, they turn a former parking space into a miniature, temporary public park.

PARK(ing) Day started in 2005 as a project of the Rebar Group, a small collective of artists, activists, and designers in San Francisco. Group members describe their motivation for the project as follows: "The great majority of San Francisco's downtown outdoor space is dedicated to movement and storage of private vehicles, while only a fraction of that space is allocated to serve a broader range of public needs" (Rebar Group 2012). Paying for a parking meter constitutes, in a sense, a short-term lease of city space, which can theoretically be used for purposes besides parking a car. PARK(ing) Day is intended to point out that fact visually and playfully, encouraging passersby to think twice about who has a right to use city spaces and for what purpose.

Although the original park(ing) spot was transformed for only a couple of hours, the idea caught on. By 2011, PARK(ing) Day organizers counted park(ing) spots in 162 cities on six continents around the world. Organizers have since declined to keep count, seeking to shift focus from numbers to the quality of the event experience. "Organizers" is a loose term in this context. Although the PARK(ing) Day movement has grown rapidly, the Rebar Group provides no hands-on logistical help for events around the world and offers only basic legal guidance for those wondering how their cities might respond to such an event. Some cities have embraced it—former San Francisco mayor Gavin Newsom gave his own personal parking spot to event planners for the day in 2006—while others have issued citations (Beale 2006). A PARK(ing) Day Manifesto is available for free download from the event website, but little else exists in the way of centralized authority or support. As the authors of *Tactical Urbanism: Short Term Change || Long Term Impact* write, "At its core, PARK(ing) Day encourages collaboration amongst local citizens to create thoughtful, but temporary additions to the public realm" (Lydon et al. 2015, 4).

Key Principles: Why It Matters to Libraries

Conditions and Causes

You might say that PARK(ing) Day isn't so much addressing a problem (even an invisible one) as it is aspiring to improve the status quo and engage the public in the life of the city. After all, from one point of view, parking spots are already doing exactly what they're supposed to—providing a space for city drivers to leave their vehicles while they shop, recreate, and more. The Rebar Group, however, would say that too much of the modern city's real estate is given over to the car and too little to green space that nurtures pedestrians.

Other motives for PARK(ing) Day include reasserting the public's right to public spaces, improving livability and liveliness on the street, and challenging the supremacy of the car. As Gretchen Coombs wrote,

> Urban interventions such as PD [PARK(ing) Day] can collapse the boundaries between art and life and use day-to-day experiences to offer new conceptions about what a "gentle" activism can elicit in the public. They raise awareness about local issues while seeking to help citizens imagine different ways of negotiating or confronting these issues through an intersection of urban design and community-based activism. (2012, 64)

PARK(ing) Day is an interesting precedent for libraries because it shows that sometimes tactical interventions can be useful even if there's no concrete problem to fix, per se. You might argue that the preponderance of car culture is a very big problem indeed (and a very complex one to solve), or that it's an invisible problem because we so often fail to think critically about how much of our shared space we've allocated to car transportation. But you could also consider PARK(ing) Day an example of a tactical intervention that simply seeks to improve the status quo. We need parking spaces—but do we need as many of them as we currently have? We need cars—but do we need to dedicate as many of our resources to them as we currently do?

When we're not grappling with invisible, complicated, and complex problems, we librarians might consider how the "gentle" activism of PARK(ing) Day could help create change in the library setting. What entrenched, accepted ideas about libraries, librarians, literacy, and community could we playfully, meaningfully challenge? What assumptions could we invite ourselves and our users to reconsider?

The Nature of the Intervention

The Rebar Group saw an imbalance in their city—too much room for cars, not enough room for people. They didn't have the authority to make policy changes about how city property was used, and they knew that changing the City of San Francisco's land use regulations would take a long time and require resources they didn't have. Rather than do nothing, they chose to highlight their concerns by staging an intervention or installation (you decide which) that was playful, low-cost, and ephemeral. By taking a humorous, flamboyant approach to the problem, they caught the attention of the public and generated the seeds of a larger movement. Like Janette Sadik-Khan, they asked forgiveness rather than permission.

Although the individual site of any PARK(ing) spot lasts just a few hours, the movement itself has longevity and international reach. From its roots in San Francisco, the event now calls attention to urbanization and land use policies in cities around the world. In a sense, the actual installation of Astroturf and picnic benches isn't the point. What makes PARK(ing) Day a success is its *decentralized, inclusive community*. Anyone can participate in the event, and the Rebar Group makes the threshold as low as possible by providing free documentation and how-to guides.

If the point of PARK(ing) Day were to permanently replace parking spots with lawns, it would be a clear failure. But that's not the point—instead, the event challenges people's perceptions of urban space and what constitutes "legitimate" use of the city. In a sense this project is even more ambitious than trying to get the City of San Francisco to build more parks because it asks everyone—business owners, pedestrians, city officials, tourists—to recognize and reconsider their own assumptions. PARK(ing) Day values this intangible outcome, as well as other intangibles such as *fostering a sense of fun*, enjoying a lively day with coconspirators, engaging in conversation and play, and *forming new relationships*.

TACTICAL URBANISM CASE STUDY 4: "SELF-GENTRIFICATION" IN THE SOUTH BRONX

THE NEIGHBORHOODS OF NEW YORK CITY'S SOUTH BRONX HAVE LONG BEEN neglected. Populated mainly by working-class minorities since the 1950s, the area was gradually abandoned by city government (and victimized by city policies) until by the 1970s it was nationally renowned as a site of urban decay. Property values plummeted after the construction of the Cross Bronx Expressway, a major freeway that not only demolished hundreds of homes but also cut straight through the borough. Crime, gang violence, and poverty rates spiked.

Landlords and homeowners, faced with seemingly irreversible losses, took to arson—the so-called Bronx Cookout—in order to collect insurance claims. Combined with fire department closures and widespread property abandonment, this practice led to a literal conflagration. According to the *New York Post*, "Seven different census tracts in The Bronx lost more than 97 percent of their buildings to fire and abandonment between 1970 and 1980; 44 tracts (out of 289 in the borough) lost more than 50 percent" (Flood 2010). The famous phrase "The Bronx is burning" cemented the reputation of the Bronx of the 1960s and 1970s as a lawless and embattled neighborhood.

In fact, many of the buildings that burned, crumbled, or collected dust in the Bronx were beautiful and highly desirable monuments—the kind of art deco and art nouveau edifices that would someday become multi-million-dollar properties. This fact didn't escape Majora Carter, who was born in the South Bronx in 1966. Carter grew up during some of the borough's toughest years, but after attending Wesleyan University she chose to return to her neighborhood. There she observed a common phenomenon—after decades of economic disinvestment, upwardly mobile people of color like her had left their South Bronx homes and businesses behind, only to see white people and developers start moving back in, benefiting from the now-historic infrastructure. As Carter said in an interview with *Slate* magazine,

> [T]he smart, hard-working kids were taught to measure success by how far we got away from our community. . . . So . . . when others are looking at our community, and going, "Oh, that's a development opportunity." We are the first ones to say, "Oh, sure. I'll sell it to you for next to nothing because you must be stupid if you see any value in this." Whereas they are thinking about the long game. And instead, we are thinking about, "We just need to get out of this place because it's so horrible." (Sheir, n.d.)

Carter found herself looking for ways to short-circuit the vicious gentrification cycle. She adopted the term *self-gentrification* to describe economic development by and for the people of color already living in poor and disadvantaged communities. Working with a series of community development corporations and nonprofits, Carter began tackling a range of problems in the South Bronx. Within a few years she had helped create a community park on a neglected stretch of the Bronx River; built advocacy partnerships against the borough's sewage treatment, power production, and freight truck traffic industries; and begun working to create local jobs. Although her advocacy work wasn't without some controversy—later in her career she was criticized for the perception that she'd moved too far from her neighborhood roots—her impact was undeniable.

In 2012 Carter founded StartUp Box South Bronx, an employment agency that focuses on getting South Bronx residents into jobs in the technology and knowledge sectors. In partnership with Mayor Bill de Blasio's Digital.NYC initiative, the start-up began providing quality assurance for video game developers. Local video gamers subcontracted through StartUp Box to play apps and games in development and document any bugs. *Wired* magazine described it as "a way of tackling the area's massive unemployment problem, while simultaneously giving the tech start-ups down in Manhattan an alternative to the inefficient and often low-quality testing services they find overseas" (Lapowski 2014).

Carter's multipronged, "self-gentrifying" work in the South Bronx, though not exactly the same as seed-bombing empty lots, shares its core DNA with the scrappy, creative enterprise of tactical urban interventions. The unorthodox and tactical nature of her approach became more obvious than ever in 2016, when she partnered with high-end New York café franchise Birch Coffee to open a coffee shop just down the street from StartUp Box South Bronx.

Pulling shots and serving macchiatos may seem like a strange career move for a MacArthur Fellowship–winning environmental and community advocate. But Carter sees the coffee shop as an important piece of the self-gentrification puzzle—a symbol of belief in the community, an affordable luxury for people without access to many others, and a marker of economic investment. Speaking to *Slate*, she said, "We've done hundreds and hundreds of surveys where we've asked people, 'What kind of stuff do you want to see in your community? What would keep you from leaving?' And people were like, 'Well, it'd be kind of nice to have a place that's not a dingy community center. . . . 'And so we built this beautiful little coffee shop" (Sheir, n.d.).

Sociologists and urban planners would call the South Bronx Birch Coffee a "third place"—an informal space where neighbors can gather at little or no cost for socializing and conversation. Writing about Carter's enterprise, the *New York Times* comments that a coffee shop "can be a community hub and a tinderbox of creativity," which is clearly Carter's intention (Gordinier 2016). And though a single high-end coffee shop—even one down the block from a tech start-up employment agency—can't turn everything around in a tough neighborhood, it's a powerful statement of optimism, ambition, and belief in a shared upward trajectory.

Key Principles: Why It Matters to Libraries

Conditions and Causes

For decades, the South Bronx has been reluctant host to a series of frustrating and damaging social problems. From redlined real estate to defunded education and social welfare services, from community-gutting expressways to a disproportionate number of toxic industries, the South Bronx has been hurt repeatedly by economic and policy decisions made elsewhere. Taken individually, these problems might be something that a community could fight and overcome. But together, they spell a larger kind of problem—a willful or ignorant disregard for the health of the community. As Majora Carter and other activists observe, class and race play a major role in the fate of the South Bronx. Social injustice isn't a history lesson but an everyday reality for many Americans and their communities.

Although Carter and other South Bronx residents face plenty of complicated and complex problems, they also face another distinctive kind of problem—the so-called wicked problem. The term was coined by social policy professors Horst Rittel and Melvin Webber at the University of California, Berkeley. Rittel and Webber maintained that standard scientific approaches couldn't deal with social policy problems because such problems weren't "tame," meaning among other things that they were impossible to definitively pin down and describe, that they involved large economic stakes, that they were connected to other types of problems, and that they involved the behavior, beliefs, and attitudes of many people. Rather than "evil" or "sinful," *wicked* in this sense refers to the problems that are inherently hard to solve.

Wicked problems are often related to planning and policy. Immigration, health care, gun control, election policies—these are all familiar examples. They all illustrate just how difficult it is to solve wicked problems because they have no definitive, predictable solution. Whereas we find complex problems hard to pin down because they change and adapt, we find wicked problems hard to solve because they address moral or philosophical questions. Wicked problems ask us to settle on a judgment or decision between good and bad, rather than a definitive finding of true or false.

When Majora Carter began her career as an environmental advocate for the South Bronx, the area was disproportionately rife with toxic landfills, power stations, and transport distribution centers—and not by accident. Decades of NIMBY (Not In My Back Yard) politics in other city boroughs led there. Generations of voters and officials in Manhattan and Brooklyn decided that they didn't want pollution, truck traffic, and electrical towers in their own neighborhoods, and instead chose to site them in the South Bronx, which lacked a cohesive, informed, activated population to fight back. Again, it's no coincidence that the South Bronx was (and is) almost entirely black and Hispanic, with one of the lowest per-capita incomes in the state. With or without specific ill intent, assumptions and opinions about race, class, and privilege have helped create wicked problems for South Bronx residents for decades.

Compared to the struggles of the South Bronx, the wicked problems facing libraries might seem trivial. But some of those problems are serious and worth considering. Hostile voters, acting on their political beliefs, can defund public libraries. Changes to how people access books and music (and how they own, share, and use them) can challenge libraries to meet expectations and stay relevant. As societies adapt to new technologies, laws, and opportunities, libraries must be alert to macro-level problems that require them to be equally adaptable.

The Nature of the Intervention

Carter's work in the South Bronx is the epitome of *local solutions for local challenges*. The problems facing the South Bronx might originate in large part outside the area, in the offices of corporations and government agencies, but their solutions cannot be wholly imported. This isn't to say that Carter and other community advocates shouldn't expect contributions from partners outside the area—these are clearly essential too. But much of Carter's credibility in Hunts Point comes from the fact that she was born and raised there and is intimately acquainted with both its problems and its potential. An intervention from the outside—from a well-intentioned corporation or nonprofit, or even the city itself—couldn't draw the same *energy and engagement from the community*. And it couldn't be as meaningful or as motivating for the people of Hunts Point to see an outsider's intervention succeed as it has been to see the success and recognition of one of their own.

Closely connected to the power of local solutions is the fact that Carter formed *partnerships with diverse individuals and groups*, making connections and talking to people in person about what she imagined and wanted for the neighborhood. Urban planner Mike Lydon, speaking about the problem of NIMBY-ism, comments that the people who participate and make themselves heard in traditional urban planning venues (neighborhood association meetings, for instance) are often already privileged and in favor of slow, conservative approaches. Expanding that group to include working-class people, people of color, young people, and others takes work, but it's worth it to include everyone. Lydon says,

> If we actually include demonstration projects as part of the public process, then we're able to meet people where they already are in their daily lives. . . . I think that's particularly important for people who are working very long hours, or working multiple shifts, and they just don't have time or even the interest to be involved civically in the decisions that get made at the city level that also impact them. (Segarra 2015)

Working with nonprofits and community development corporations, and later with her own employment agency and coffee shop start-ups, Carter was able to engage members of the South Bronx community who weren't aware of or included in such traditional urban planning processes as weekday hearings, town hall meetings, and public comment periods.

Carter's venture into entrepreneurship with Birch Coffee may seem like an odd choice for a world-changing activist, but it fits perfectly with a tactical mind-set that values *creativity, optimism, and delight*. A great neighborhood is not made from policies and parks alone. Urban planners and designers have long recognized that people value amenities, including diverse and independent retail districts, clean and safe sidewalks, and, yes, even nice coffee shops. Some might consider it frivolous to offer a three-dollar cup of coffee to a neighborhood struggling to get decent schools and health care. But as Carter asks, "Why is it there is this [perception] that people in low-status communities don't like or deserve nice things? They do!" (Sheir, n.d.). People in the neighborhood have responded accordingly.

Carter's projects also created and identified value in the *social capital and relationships between individuals and agencies*. Carter's multipronged work crosses boundaries—from environmental advocacy to social justice to job creation to her leap into the private sector with Birch Coffee. In each of these ventures she built relationships that helped establish her in the community and beyond it. The New York Times comments that Carter "is so well known that there is a painted mural of her face mounted on a fence not far from the coffee shop," pointing out not just her local roots but the immense social capital she's built (Gordinier 2016). Carter herself explicitly recognizes the importance of intangible relationships in building a better neighborhood. Talking to Slate magazine, she suggests words she'd like to see used to describe her work: "Build. [Laughs] Transform. Love. These are words I use all the time as we speak about community building and even real estate development because these are the kind of communities, like, we want to show you don't have to move out of your neighborhood to live in a better one" (Sheir, n.d.).

SOME USEFUL URBANISM CONCEPTS

URBAN PLANNERS AND designers have developed many core concepts that can be very useful to librarians. Here are a few key ideas to consider in your library:

Placemaking: The idea of a "place" may be one of the most abstract ideas we have, but it's also one we rely on inherently to make sense of the world. Placemaking is the process we use to tame, name, and understand our surroundings—to make a fundamentally hostile world more pleasant and livable. Lynda Schneekloth and Robert Shibley define placemaking as "both daily acts of renovating, maintaining, and representing the spaces that sustain us, and of special, celebratory one-time events such as designing a new church building or moving into a new facility" (1995, 1). We all participate in placemaking, but architects and urban planners are professional placemakers who take special care to understand how and why people create and exist in certain types of places. We can borrow some of their wisdom in the library context, where understanding placemaking can help us plan and improve our physical spaces and possibly even our digital ones. In the physical world of the library, placemaking would have us prioritize human needs and preferences such as clear wayfinding, daylight and friendly artificial light, and pleasing, coherent design schemes. In the digital world, those priorities can translate into web design that makes affordances for eye fatigue and values delightful details such as skillful color palettes and well-designed fonts. We recognize and associate places with certain qualities, positive or negative, because of these characteristics, whether we know it or not. It's why we make jokes about waiting in line at the DMV (a famously human-hostile environment) and use photos of lofty, classical libraries as our computer desktops. We can use an understanding of placemaking to make our libraries into places where everyone wants to be.

Design Thinking: This may sound like a pretty abstract, catch-all term, but in fact it refers to a specific and structured approach to identifying and solving problems. The method has roots in the 1987 urban design book *Design Thinking* by Harvard professor Peter Rowe. Design thinking solves problems by following a defined set of steps in a certain order: usually a team works to understand the user's experience, then define the problem, generate a large number of potential solutions to the problem, physically prototype solutions, and, finally, test those prototypes. Over time this method has been adapted for use across design and business fields, in management consulting, and even in higher education. In library settings, design thinking is a powerful tool for articulating complex and wicked problems, generating staff engagement, and building and rewarding empathy, creativity, and innovation. Renowned design firm IDEO has partnered with the Bill and Melinda Gates Foundation to create a web-based tool kit for design thinking in libraries, available at http://designthinkingforlibraries.com/.

Charrette: A charrette is the architect's time-honored way of sharing and testing ideas with clients and other stakeholders. It's essentially an intense meeting with clearly defined goals, at which designers as well as other stakeholders (citizens, funders, government officials, etc.) are led by a trained facilitator to share ideas and come to agreement on a direction for the project. Key to the charrette is that all participants are there to contribute—the charrette process is a way of teasing out ideas, opinions, and values from everyone involved. In a library setting, a charrette is an excellent way to collect ideas before you renovate your space or build something new. A charrette might also be a good model for gathering input about special new projects and partnerships—for learning what your users, potential and existing partners, staff, and administrators think before you take the plunge. Charrettes serve to inspire as well as to engage, so gathering your stakeholders for an intensive, disciplined discussion can be worthwhile in other situations too.

Pink Zones and Innovation Districts: These ideas are relatively new in the urbanism world. Pink zones are neighborhoods in which land use and zoning procedural red tape is loosened to make it easier to try new things. The country's first pink zone is in Detroit, Michigan, a city in great need of streamlined processes for urban experimentation. Examples of pink zoning include easing restrictions on different types of buildings, making investment easier for developers, and reworking building codes. Innovation districts are neighborhoods where the zoning and building codes specifically encourage the development of high-tech, cutting-edge, and creative start-ups and firms. Cities like Seattle, Philadelphia, and Oklahoma City have created innovation districts to attract high-tech corporations and foster their technology job markets. The focus in innovation districts is on economic and talent development, especially in high-growth industries, while the focus in pink zones includes community development, small business, and housing. Both offer intriguing precedents for libraries—can designating a distinct physical or virtual space for innovation in your library change your operations or your output? Can you argue for a temporary "pink zone" where rules are lessened or lightened for a trial period?

Optical Leverage: In *City: Rediscovering the Center*, urbanist and researcher William Whyte described the way that seeing people sitting down and eating (in outdoor cafés, for instance) will draw more people to sit and eat. He wrote, "The optical leverage in these things is tremendous. For basic props, nothing more is needed than several stacks of chairs and tables, and a canvas awning or two. Spread them out, put up the umbrellas, bring on the waitresses and the customers, and the visual effect can be stunning . . . . Food, to repeat, draws people, who draw more people." (1988, 142–143). It's common sense, but Whyte was one of the first people to point out this fact, and it holds true for activities besides eating. If you want people to come into your library and read (or game or hula-hoop), make sure they can see people inside reading (or gaming or hula-hooping). Big windows, glass doors, patio seating, open-air foyers—how else can you reveal what's going on inside your library?

"Liked" Environments: Urban planners pay special attention to the types of places that people like to be in—the ones they're drawn to even if they don't have to go to them. At Ohio State University, Professor Jack Nasar developed a short list of characteristics of what he called liked environments. These included some element of nature (versus wholly man-made), clear evidence of upkeep (the space is cared for), a mixture of openness and defined space (meaning a blend of open space and panoramic views), clear historical significance (presuming this has a favorable connotation), and order (a sense of congruence, coherence, and clarity). Some of Nasar's findings align with other, older theories such as "prospect and refuge" (see later in this feature) which suggests that humans are most comfortable in spaces where they have access to both a long view and a protected space. Urban designers rely on these concepts to create pleasing parks, streets, and neighborhoods—but they can be valuable tools for library design as well. Does your library have daylight, plants, or any other element of nature? Can patrons curl up in a carrel with a view of the reading room, or do your chairs face the periodicals shelves? Is the library tidy and well organized? If your building has historic elements, can you expose and highlight them? Even in a new building, this can sometimes be possible—consider adding a so-called truth window to your new building project to offer users a glimpse inside the working walls.

Third Place: The idea of the "third place" comes from sociology. If the "first place" is home and the "second place" is work, the "third place" is anywhere that people gather to socialize, share information, and feel at home. Usually third places have a negligible or zero cost of entry, allowing community members to congregate regardless of income level. Third places are usually informal, open to all, and populated by regulars. Many third places offer food and drink to create a convivial atmosphere. Some classic examples of third places include barbershops and beauty parlors; cafés, bars, and pubs; neighborhood parks; bookstores; and libraries. In these settings, people are able to engage in conversation across social boundaries in ways they can't at work or at home. The social interactions fostered in these spaces may be hard to quantify, but they have qualitative value. Just as tactical urbanists take care to articulate the value of intangibles such as social capital, librarians should point out the distinctive nature of library spaces and the relationships they can foster. Where else can college students talk vinyl with retirees, and stay-at-home dads get infant tips from new-immigrant parents? The library is a great natural collocator. How can you enhance your library's inherent ability to bring people together? How can you facilitate more boundary-crossing and more sharing of civil leisure time?

Prospect and Refuge: This handy concept comes not only from urban design but from landscape architecture, art history, and even evolutionary psychology. It suggests that human beings prefer to be in landscapes that offer a long panorama of their surroundings, combined with a secure spot from which to view those surroundings. In other words, people like to see without necessarily being seen. The idea was proposed by British geographer Jay Appleton who, in his 1975 book The Experience of Landscape, suggested that these opposing desires reflect the combined human needs for opportunity and safety. Appleton's argument was aesthetic, but his idea has been adopted by architects and urban designers to create environments that make people feel comfortable and stimulated at the same time. In a library setting, consider whether your physical space offers patrons and staff the ability both to see what's going on around them (who's coming and going, what's happening outside) and to retreat from being observed. You might spend some time watching to see which study carrels or seats your patrons choose to occupy first and most—are they the ones in the central, exposed areas of your library, or the ones by the walls and in the corners? What happens if you change your furniture around, or offer mobile wall panels, or change your lighting scheme?

SLOAP: SLOAP is an acronym for Space Left Over After Planning. It refers to the unclaimed, often oddly shaped bits and pieces of space left in the urban environment after buildings, parks, and streets are made. From a standard planning perspective, SLOAP is often considered useless and unsightly, a product of an imperfect process. From a tactical urbanist perspective, SLOAP can be highly valuable. It can provide incubator sites to try new ideas without rigorous opposition from regulators or competitors for the space. SLOAP is also often small, making it more feasible for grassroots experimentation. Janette Sadik-Khan took advantage of SLOAP-style "snippets" of land in New York City to create "parklets," like the DUMBO park, which were individually small but collectively meaningful in creating livable neighborhoods. In Bangkok, real estate developer AP Thailand turned small, angular lots into popular nonregulation soccer pitches (Brownlee 2016). In a library setting, look for unused corners that can be adopted for creative repurposing. What about a Little Free Library in a corner of the break room, or a multipronged device charger at that awkward elbow in the reference desk? What's in the library's foyer or its stairwell? What small, ungainly space can you reclaim for a creative new purpose?

New Urbanism: By the end of the twentieth century, Western architecture and urban design had passed through a series of trends, including modernism, the International style, the garden city movement, urban renewal, and postmodernism. Some of these movements resulted in monolithic buildings that were awkwardly situated in existing pre-WWII street plans and city design, making for unapproachable, disorienting, and overwhelming landscapes (see also SLOAP). New Urbanism developed in the 1980s as an antidote: a return to walkable, human-scale neighborhoods with legible centers and boundaries, narrow streets, local businesses and other infrastructure, the preservation of older human-scaled buildings, and a range of mixed-age housing to accommodate rich and poor, young and old. In other words, New Urbanism is an urban planning movement focused on the everyday needs of people rather than on monumental architecture. Libraries can take a leaf from the New Urbanist book by examining their spaces (inside and out) through library users' eyes. How easy is it to find the library's front door? What's most eye-catching when you enter? Is signage clear and simple, both large enough to read and low enough for children or wheelchair users to see? Do users have to visit more than one desk to accomplish an everyday task? Can parents and responsible adults easily supervise the children's area? A New Urbanist library design prioritizes the users' most ordinary activities because they're the ones that make up the fabric of everyday life.

3

A REALISTIC TACTICAL APPROACH

OW THAT WE'VE SPENT SOME TIME STUDYING EXAMPLES OF tactical urbanism, I hope your curiosity is piqued to see how these same approaches can succeed in different types of library work. Before we do that, let's quickly review some of the characteristics we've isolated and take a minute to ground ourselves in the potential pitfalls and realistic requirements of any tactical intervention.

Tactical urbanism is defined by more than just a roll-up-your-sleeves, hands-on approach to problems. As we've seen, characteristics of tactical urbanism include:

- Cultivating a willingness to experiment—and to fail. (Or to "fail," because testing an idea that won't work can give you more information about what might.)
- Fostering charm, playfulness, delight, and humor—and letting them work for you.
- Engaging with and informing your community members to take advantage of their skills and share ownership of the project.
- Starting small by chunking a big problem into smaller pieces, running a pilot, or testing ideas with a small group.

- Trying an approach that maximizes the value of skills and resources you do have rather than wasting time and energy on unrealistically ambitious or out-of-scope work.
- Growing bigger over time—maybe. If the resources are available and the project is right, growth might make sense. But sometimes it makes sense to stay small.
- Valuing intangible and ephemeral outcomes, sometimes as much as or more than concrete, permanent ones.
- Talking to everyone. Making documentation available for free download so projects can be replicated, designing projects to be appealing and welcoming so that people will spread the word, holding open meetings and charrettes and demonstrations so that stakeholders can share their opinions.
- Lowering the threshold for participation so that as many people as possible can join. Valuing people's presence and interest as well as their skilled contributions.
- Pursuing a "passion project." Most tactical urbanists aren't paid—in some cases they spend their own money on the work. They willingly contribute energy, time, and other resources because they care about the project and the larger goal it serves.

Okay, but What about the Pitfalls?

It would be nice to say that because a tactical approach is so nimble, flexible, and responsive, it's perfect. That no matter how you wield it or what your circumstances, it solves every problem and nothing ever goes wrong again.

Not so.

There are some valid critiques of tactical interventions, which it's important to recognize before we leap into our library case studies. Forewarned is forearmed, so here are some important questions for anyone to consider before gearing up to take a tactical, DIY, or "guerrilla" approach to libraries.

Will It Succeed?

Put another way, will it accomplish its goal? The case studies we've examined have been by and large successful in the sense that they've accomplished a larger secondary goal or have grown to include more participants over time. But it's also true that there are projects that don't transfer, grow, or last. Whether that means they're a failure depends on a lot of things. If Amtrak never showed up to fix the broken pipes in Queens, would the Astoria Scum River Bridge have been a failure? Maybe not, if it was still getting people across the puddle. Maybe so, if it demonstrated that the property owners were indifferent even to this implicit thrown gauntlet. Tactical interventions may not take much money, but they take time, energy, social capital, and other resources. Not all of them will catch on as well as the ones we've seen. Does that mean they're failures? That depends on your goals and your point of view. You'll need to consider both before you start your intervention and communicate them to your stakeholders so that everyone has realistic expectations and understands what success looks like.

Will It Build Goodwill?

We might all like the idea of more green space, pedestrian safety, and human-scaled spaces in our cities. But when you're trying to park your car outside the day care and all the spots are covered in Astroturf and picnic tables, you might not have a lot of patience for the big-picture goals of reenvisioning urban land use. Tactical interventions are, to varying degrees but by their very nature, provocative. Even when they're employed within the official power structure—think of Sadik-Khan's improvised DUMBO parklet—they partake of the spirit of activism and gadfly-ism. This can be a good thing if your goal is to gently nudge authority into action. It can also be a problem if your project increases intransigence—or worse, if it alienates the community you seek to engage.

Is It Legal?

Again by their very nature, tactical interventions often skirt the edges of what's legal or allowed. By definition, a tactical approach is at least complementary or supplementary to a larger strategy and its processes—and, depending on the situation, it may operate subversively, outside official structures completely. Tactical interventions often challenge the very definition of "legal" by engaging in activities that nobody's tried before. Strictly speaking, it's probably not legal to toss seeds into an abandoned and overgrown lot, or to build a wooden footbridge and leave it on a sidewalk in Queens—but given the context of official neglect and the interventionists' larger goals, both actions probably seem justifiable. Sometimes these kinds of interventions can provoke a thoughtful response and engagement with the underlying problem. Sometimes they can provoke legal action that doesn't improve anything and might just make things worse.

How Will You Handle Criticism?

You can't please all the people all the time. For everyone who applauds the ingenuity of a hand-built foot bridge, there will be others who see it as self-serving, impractical, or even dangerous. The more provocative the intervention, the wider the range of responses is likely to be. Business owners might not love the idea of artists and activists occupying the parking spots outside their front doors without spending any money. Janette Sadik-Khan got a lot done, but she also ruffled feathers in the New York City transportation bureaucracy and gained a reputation for running roughshod over long-standing practice and policy. The hands-on, upstart nature of tactical interventions means you'll always have critics. Some of what they say may be knee-jerk opposition, and some of it may be valid feedback that can help shape your work. It will be up to you to decide what to do with the criticism you'll inevitably receive.

How Will You Know Who's in Charge—And Who'll Be in Charge Next Week?

There are upsides to bureaucracy. Bureaucracies are consistent, predictable, and stable (or they should be). One downside of leaving the bureaucracy behind is that decentralized, passion-driven organizations can be much more prone to turnover, churn, and dissolution. Depending on the nature of your project, this may not be a problem—it only takes a few weeks or days (or hours) to plan and deliver a PARK(ing) Day parklet. But for larger projects with more partners, a longer time horizon, and more ambitious goals, some kind of organizational legibility and stability will be important.

Who Will Provide What You Need?

Tactical interventions are usually low budget (or at least lower budget than full-scale strategic initiatives), but they still need stuff. Take money out of the equation and you've still got a host of other resources that drive any successful project: relationships, experience, time, skill, and more. Don't assume that because a project is low budget that it will be quick or easy to accomplish—or that it won't cost money in the end. Time is money, after all. And while we can do a great deal without a budget, it never pays to forget the bottom line.

Which brings us to . . .

A Word about Money

Sooner or later, money will come up. Probably it will happen at the beginning of your project—especially if you think you have no money (or not enough) to accomplish what you want to do. It might be as frank as a budget statement, or it might be more subtle, such as a concern about devoting work hours to a side project. Sometimes we consider money without even realizing it—we reject the possibility of trying a project before we really start to think it through because we assume it will take money we don't have. How often have you heard a colleague (or yourself) say, "Yeah, right, but doing that would take *money*."

Money is often a sore spot for librarians. Libraries, after all, are typically not revenue-generating institutions—at least not in the short term. From a strictly capitalist perspective, it's possible to see libraries as money sinks, taking annual allocations from city or university budgets and producing—what? It's hard to put a price tag on better-educated, more employable citizens and students or on happier people (although some libraries have done exactly that, providing value calculators on their websites or on lending receipts that let patrons see how much money they save each year by using the library).

In the long run, studies show that although libraries, and education in general, cost money, they are extremely beneficial to the economies that support them. Using various methods of applying concrete value to circulating collections and services, public and academic libraries have shown return on investment (ROI) rates anywhere from $1.30 to $10.00 on a dollar's investment (American Library Association, n.d.). And many cities and institutions recognize the enormous wealth—financial, social, and otherwise—represented by their library's collections, spaces, and people. Many library directors have a clear place at the table where financial decisions are made.

And yet, no matter how highly our parent institutions might regard us, there's almost always at least some way in which we don't have enough money. Maybe we can't hire all the positions we want—the new programmers to help us do great things with our mobile website, or the user experience (UX) designer to revamp our service points. Maybe we're cutting collections budgets because of inflation. Or maybe our buildings have deferred maintenance—a new carpet, updated furniture. Libraries are costly to run, precisely because we do so much. It's safe to assume we'll never have all the money we want.

In some ways, that realization may be freeing. If there's never going to be enough money to do everything we want, maybe we can start to think about how much we can accomplish anyway. After all, money accomplishes nothing on its own. Most projects take resources of many kinds—relationships, goodwill, social capital, know-how, staffing, space, institutional memory, creativity, ideas, elbow grease, and a willingness to step outside our comfort zones, to name just a few.

If we can include some of those other assets on our mental budget statements, maybe we'll feel heartened enough to get a project off the ground. We'll try a pilot or a proof of concept, or we'll do something on a tiny scale instead of a large one. As so many tactical urbanist projects show, sometimes just getting off the ground is enough. If we can show others that we're creative, scrappy, and ready to work hard, sometimes we can attract partners from unexpected places. We'll see some compelling examples of that in chapter 4, as we examine tactical interventions in libraries.

Even as we celebrate what we can do on a small (or nonexistent) budget, we should bear in mind that money will almost certainly play a role in our project at some point. A proof of concept is one thing. A fully fledged program or service is another. Remember the advice of Mike Lydon and his colleagues: "If done well, these small scale changes are conceived as the first step in realizing lasting change" (2015, 2). Painting a disused parking lot green may not take much money, but rolling out a citywide plan for urban parks does.

Still, some budget managers might balk at spending money on a pilot project that might fail or on a proof of concept that will be taken apart in six months. Their anxiety is understandable—like libraries and education, experimentation costs money up front with little or no immediate, visible, guaranteed return on investment. But from a larger, longer-term perspective, spending small amounts of money to test out ideas before committing to larger implementations is one of the smartest things an organization can do. As Mike Lydon and his colleagues go on to say,

> Indeed, there is real merit in a municipality spending $30,000 on temporary material changes before investing $3,000,000 in those that are permanent. If the improvement doesn't work as planned, the whole budget will not be shot, and future designs can continue to be calibrated to meet the needs of a particular, and dynamic context. (2017, 2)

HOW ABOUT TACTICAL BUSINESS PRACTICES?

URBAN STUDIES ISN'T the only field that values a tactical approach. Business leaders put a premium on innovation and creativity and are constantly on the lookout for ways to foster out-of-the-box thinking within organizations. Here are some of the ways in which business leaders encourage experimentation, ingenuity, and a tactical mind-set in their organizations—ways that you or your library administrator might adapt and adopt for use in your library.

Skunkworks: A *skunk works,* according to the Oxford English Dictionary, was originally "a small, freq[uently] informal group within an engineering, computing, or other company working, often in secret or in isolation from the rest of the company, on a radical and innovative project." The proprietary term—notice that it's two words—derives from the name of a specific such group at the military engineering firm Lockheed in the 1940s. Over time it's taken on broader meaning as it's spread through different industries, and the original skunk works has been contracted to a single word. But it still refers to a small group working on an innovative side project within a larger organization.

Skunkworks teams are considered good for innovation because they can work at a small, intimate scale and a rapid pace, unencumbered by the bureaucracy and competing priorities of the rest of the business. Some firms take their skunkworks secrecy more seriously than others—one of the most famously

covert skunkworks projects is Google X, the lab responsible for Google Glass and the Google driverless car.

In the library context, assigning a small team to work temporarily on radically innovative side projects can be a tactical win. Bethany Nowviskie—research associate professor of digital humanities at the University of Virginia—thinks so, at least. She styles the R&D unit within the university's Scholars' Lab as a skunkworks operation, albeit without the secrecy of Google X. Nowviskie says,

> A "skunkworks" (all one word) describes a small and nimble technical team, deliberately and self-consciously and (yes) quite unfairly freed from much of the surrounding bureaucracy of the larger organization in which it finds itself. This enviable cutting of slack and tolerance of the renegade is offset by placement, on the shoulders of the skunkworks team, of greatly raised expectations of innovation. (2011)

In Nowviskie's opinion, skunkworks are useful because they step out of the usual way of doing things just long enough to create something new that can be applied back to the larger organization's work. Take note: that application can be challenging. For all the benefits of running innovation as a side project, some managers struggle with the challenge of scaling up and sustaining skunkworks products and integrating them into the rest of the business (Richardson 2010).

Creative time and daylighting: "Creative time" refers to the corporate practice of offering employees "free time" in their schedules in order to work on creative projects, with the expectation that all employee work feeds back into the bottom line. Google is perhaps the most famous exemplar: it instituted a 20 percent creative time policy, essentially offering its staff one day a week to work on side projects. That policy has been retired, but plenty of companies have similar practices in place. Fast Company magazine notes,

> LinkedIn has InCubator, a program that gives engineers time away from their regular work to work on their own product ideas; Apple has Blue Sky, which allows some workers to spend a few weeks on pet projects; and Microsoft created The Garage, a space for employees to build their own products using Microsoft resources. (Subramanian 2013)

"Daylighting" (the opposite of "moonlighting") refers to the practice of unofficially working more than one job at a time. So if your workplace offers you "creative time," you might use it to learn to code and then apply that knowledge to build a tool that benefits your employer. On the other hand, "daylighting" might mean that you're spending your lunch breaks driving for Uber. You might assume that creative time is good, while daylighting is always bad. In fact, there are mixed opinions about both. Creative time has been criticized for everything from presenting a false picture of employer expectations—staff are hired

with the promise of free creative time, only to find the corporate culture so demanding that they can hardly keep up with their jobs—to failing to deliver the innovation it seeks. And daylighting has been seen by some as a valuable way to engage millennial talent and help ambitious people earn more (Behance 2009).

In a library context, it may be worth supporting the enthusiasm of creative, driven employees by offering some flexibility in official position descriptions and schedules. And because the private sector is increasingly embracing the reality of daylighting, maybe libraries should too. Consider the approach of design giant IDEO, which regularly arranges "'white space projects'—tasks as varied as event planning or data visualization, which employees from any department can join in on" (Subramanian 2013). If library staff have passions and competencies outside their job descriptions, maybe the library can put them to good use.

Design sprints: Sometimes you want to put an idea to the test without carrying it all the way to fruition. Maybe the project would cost too much to implement without more testing, or maybe you can learn everything you need to know without committing to the product. Maybe you just need answers quickly. One tactic to try is a design sprint—a proprietary process developed by GV, a former subsidiary of Google and Alphabet. Design sprints are intensive, weeklong, phased processes that build on the principles of design thinking (see the definition of that term in the chapter 2 feature titled "Some Useful Urbanism

Concepts"). In a typical design sprint, a small team of designers and innovators follows a carefully structured process to identify a challenge, engage expert opinions, suggest and test solutions, create a prototype, and gather feedback on their ideas. The tactical advantages of the approach include a low cost threshold, a rapid iterative process, and full opportunity for local experts and users to engage in the project. Companies such as Nest and Medium have used design sprints, as have libraries such as the Suffolk library system in England and universities such as the University of Mary Washington and the University of Florida (Clearleft 2005; Bessette 2016; Innovation Academy 2016). In a library context, it might make sense to appoint one or two staff members to learn more about design thinking and the design sprint tactic, then try a weeklong sprint the next time you're considering tackling a new project.

Do (or Think-and-Do) Tanks: You're probably familiar with the concept of the "think tank," which is a group of experts charged with developing opinions, advice, and ideas on a given topic. A Do Tank (or a Think-and-Do Tank) tweaks that concept—instead of just pondering trends or concepts, Do Tank members come up with actionable ideas and then find ways to put them into practice. This might sound like common sense, but it represents a shift in thinking from past generations of political and corporate advisory bodies. Companies such as LeadLocal and DoTank offer consultation services to help organizations move from contemplation to action, coaching teams on how to research, interview, connect, and tell their stories better. These organizations focus on local solutions to challenges and make use of design thinking and prototyping. Lawrence MacDonald and Todd Moss (2014) of the Center for Global Development published principles for a successful Do Tank, advising leaders to share ideas and ownership, distribute responsibility, experiment, and value intangibles like social engagement and enjoyment. Sound familiar?

In a library context, consider reexamining the role of whatever committees or advisory groups currently serve as think tanks for the organization. Can those groups reposition themselves in more active roles in the organization? Can the organization's leaders and advisors find ways to move from contemplation to action?

4

LIBRARY CASE STUDIES

IBRARIANS HAVE EVERYTHING IN COMMON WITH THE ART-
ists, activists, civil servants, and ordinary citizens who
practice tactical urbanism. As much as librarianship is a
staid, conservative, and traditional profession, it's also a
profession of activists and idealists. So it should come as
no surprise that there are already examples of librarians taking innovative
and tactical approaches to problem solving in libraries all over the world.

In this chapter and the next, we'll look at some examples of how librarians have taken a tactical approach to solving problems and creating
change. We'll see projects from a wide range of library work, from library
systems to advocacy to technical services to space planning. We'll also follow up on some of these projects, talking to the librarians who led them
about why they took action and what they learned—as well as how successful the project has been and how the work is going now.

TACTICAL LIBRARY CASE STUDY 1: LIBRARYBOX

BY NOW, WIRELESS INTERNET SEEMS UBIQUITOUS IN AMERICA. A 2015 STUDY BY
the Pew Research Center indicates that 68 percent of Americans now own

smartphones, a number that actually seems low given how many people seem to be constantly engaged with their e-mail, Facebook, and other social media accounts (Mediati 2015).

And yet there are still places without quality wireless connections—often the places that seem to need it most. Many networks are slow, low capacity, or burdened by filters and firewalls. Any librarian who's taught in the basement classroom of a 1960s-era concrete library building can speak to the problem of gaps in our wireless coverage. Any librarian who's had a creative program idea foiled by the absence of a wireless network at a public park, church, or swimming hole can do the same. And outside the industrialized world, there are many places where Internet access is disrupted, censored, unreliable, monitored, or simply nonexistent—places where people can't share or access needed information.

Although most of us take wireless networks for granted, when we start to probe more closely, we discover that they're complex technical systems often backed by corporations with whose politics we may not agree. Librarians typically want their patrons to enjoy privacy and intellectual freedom, but some network providers may prioritize data gathering, traffic throttling, and profit maximizing. Librarians may feel frustrated that they can't take more control over their networks, extending them into new locations or changing their coverage as needed. They may feel overwhelmed and intimidated by the alphabet soup of network protocols or the cost of equipment and personnel. They may want to set their own policies and share their own hyperlocal collections with library users.

Jason Griffey took on all these concerns when he created the first LibraryBox as a proof of concept in 2012. A LibraryBox is essentially a router and a flash drive that can be used to set up a small, private, anonymous network for file sharing, chat, and more. LibraryBoxen (the official plural) are driven by open-source code and a small amount of power, such as what's available from computers, solar panels, or bike dynamos. A LibraryBox provides a private, anonymous network that doesn't track any user information and isn't connected to the greater Internet. It essentially offers a tiny, portable, local Internet sharing just what you put on it.

After unveiling the first device at the 2012 Computers in Libraries conference, Griffey went on to refine his idea and launch a Kickstarter campaign at the 2013 American Library Association Annual Conference. The funds he raised helped to produce LibraryBox 2.0, a more easily reproduced version of the technology that included responsive web design and more internationally available hardware choices. The Kickstarter campaign also showed the library community's eagerness to support the project—it was fully funded in six hours and went on to raise over $30,000, many times Griffey's modest target. Author and technology critic Cory Doctorow took notice and helped promote the project on the popular Boing Boing website, driving even more attention Griffey's way.

In true developer style, Griffey followed LibraryBox 2.0 with yet another iteration, LibraryBox 2.1. This time, the project was awarded a Knight Foundation Prototype Grant, and the device found its way into a wide range of uses. Some were relatively predictable—public libraries preloading LibraryBoxen with public domain e-content to share at outreach events, teachers using LibraryBoxen in classrooms with poor connectivity. Others were more unusual—scientists at the Monterey Bay Aquarium toted LibraryBoxen to remote Pacific Islands to share digital libraries of scholarly articles with colleagues in the field, and a city in France used a LibraryBox to provide digital information to people waiting at a bus stop.

Because the LibraryBox is not connected to the larger Internet, it's impossible to monitor exactly how and where the devices are in play, but as of 2015 the user community reported LibraryBoxen in thirty-three American states, thirty-seven countries, and six continents. Australian librarians use LibraryBoxen to take e-content to remote rural communities in the Outback. A librarian uses LibraryBoxen aboard the Story Sailboat, a boat-based delivery method for library services in the San Francisco Bay area. International aid workers use LibraryBoxen to distribute health and nursing information in rural areas of Africa, where people have mobile phones but no stable Internet connection.

Griffey spent 2015 as a Berkman Fellow at Harvard University's Berkman Klein Center for Internet and Society, where he continued to promote the LibraryBox project and improve it technologically. Future iterations of the LibraryBox might include an open education curriculum for mobile deployment. The ultimate goal of the project is to make it easier and cheaper for people to control the information they need.

Key Principles: How It Speaks to Tactical Urbanism

Conditions and Causes

The problem of spotty or limited wireless is familiar to many of us in the developed world, but it rarely rises to the level of a true crisis. Most often, we make do with dead zones and slow connections—or we supplement weak public networks with our private, paid access to Internet on our smartphones. It's a lot easier than tackling the larger problems of inadequate hardware, narrow bandwidth, poor customer service from network providers, or IT staff with too much on their plates.

Similarly, we might not like the fact that corporations control our access to information on the Internet or that they might be tracking our patrons, but it's hard to imagine building our own Internet instead. Network providers are some of the largest, most powerful companies in the world, and policies surrounding their actions are set at the highest levels. The service they provide is bound to expensive infrastructure and complex technology.

For all these reasons, imperfect Internet access can be the kind of invisible problem that we just decide to live with. It's not in our job description—or anyone's, it seems—to fix systemic technological or policy problems. In fact, some people might not even see these as problems at all, but merely as the status quo. Of course we care about access and privacy—but most of us in areas with mostly stable networks are too busy doing the rest of our jobs to worry about tackling this huge, complex, and mostly invisible problem.

The Nature of the Intervention

Faced with a set of challenges familiar to many urban activists, the LibraryBox project took a distinctly tactical approach to solving them. No one librarian could hope to re-create the web. Instead, Jason Griffey "broke off a piece of the Internet," as he describes it, and got to work on improving that. Like Jason Eppink and Posterchild contemplating the sidewalk puddle in Astoria, Queens, Griffey had neither the resources nor the time to rebuild what he saw as a broken (or at least imperfect) network infrastructure. Rather than try to do that, he *concentrated on a smaller part of the problem*—creating a portable, anonymous mini-network. Chunked into smaller pieces, the problem was much more manageable.

Although Griffey founded LibraryBox alone, *partnerships* have been key to the project's success. Even his initial proof of concept was based (with consent) on the work of another technologist, David Darts. From that point, Griffey consciously sought out the attention and contributions of librarians, teachers, coders, and others interested in the device. Some partners supplied technological know-how, while others provided social networks, access to new user groups, or funding to help the project grow.

As an open source project, LibraryBox is similar to PARK(ing) Day in that everyone is encouraged to take part in their own way and make the project their own. The barriers to entry are low and getting lower with every new iteration of the code and hardware. Librarians without technology training can still easily manage the router, USB drive, and browser that make up the LibraryBox end user experience. And though Griffey imagined the tool for library and classroom use, it's found applications and a *decentralized community of users* around the world.

Like some of the best (and quirkiest) tactical urbanist interventions, LibraryBox has an element of the *passion project*. Griffey conceived of the device after seeing David Darts's precedent, itself as much a work of art as a practical tool for sharing information. He developed the proof of concept out of his own interest and shared it at a professional conference, rather than as part of a formal workplace assignment. In other words, LibraryBox was born from creativity and ingenuity as much as from a desire to solve a real-world problem. Without that spirit of can-do excitement, the project would never have gotten off the ground, much less gone on to travel the world.

Following Up: An Interview with Jason Griffey

I TALKED WITH Jason Griffey, Fellow at the Berkman Klein Center for Internet and Society at Harvard University and creator of the LibraryBox, about rural connectivity, copyright rebels, and eureka moments.

Why was the LibraryBox project important to you?

I grew up in eastern Kentucky and throughout the rural south. The rurality of America is something I was very concerned about from a library infrastructure point of view. I saw both a lack of robust infrastructure and the lack of hope for any to be created, because there wasn't enough density to warrant anyone caring about it in any significant way.

As I talked to librarians in those areas I kept seeing a need for something to address this problem. My interest in making technologies kept overlapping with my ambient awareness of this need and eventually with a project I'd been following for a while called PirateBox. PirateBox was developed by an art professor at New York University, David Darts. He created it as an art piece and saw it as an anti-copyright piece for sharing content. It was rebellious in nature—it was in a black lunch box with a skull and crossbones on it, very visually interesting.

What's the problem you were trying to solve with LibraryBox?

My original thought was that librarians would use it to take content out into the world, like a digital bookmobile—to farmers' markets and library pop-ups and things like that. When I took the first box to Computers in Libraries, I loaded it with my presentation and slides. That was an obvious use, that hyperlocal delivery of content to an individual or a classroom.

I hadn't yet come around to understanding that in many places there is infrastructure but it's so controlled or restricted that it's like not having any. Or that LibraryBox could be used to bypass censorship or provide access to materials that had been restricted by local government or an institution. That censorship angle hadn't occurred to me in 2012.

But it wasn't long after I published my website that I was contacted by an English teacher in China who was using LibraryBox to provide English-language materials her students couldn't get to because of the Great Firewall. That was another explosion in my head. In a situation where the network is monitored or controlled, LibraryBox provides access at point of need. It has not only an educational bent but an activist or social justice bent as well. That was thrilling.

How did you get the idea for LibraryBox in particular?

I have an interest in how copyright is held and/or shared and/or ignored in the U.S., so I'd been watching PirateBox. In 2011 or 2012 a couple of coders took Darts's original idea, simplified it, and ported it to less expensive hardware. His original installation was more involved, heavier, it required big batteries. They simplified it. When I saw this it set off lightbulbs above my head. It was a eureka moment.

Because all of this code was open source and because the hardware costs were so low, it was inexpensive to test and play with the PirateBox idea. I took their code and made a fork and played around with the interface. I didn't have a huge list of things I needed to do to make this more comfortable for libraries to use. It just needed to be easier to use and have a few user interface changes. So I just started to work on that.

I built the first LibraryBox as a proof of concept at my kitchen table. I took it with me to the Computers in Libraries conference in 2012 and just said, I built this thing. What do you think? I showed it to friends and they all thought it was really cool. I could see their excitement about its potential and that's when I thought yeah, maybe this has legs.

I thought I was building something that a few libraries here and there would use. You never know how it's going to go. But that was the genesis of it, this very interesting eureka moment that was a combo of all these other things I had in my head.

How did people respond to LibraryBox?

So far I've only heard from people who like it. I haven't been vilified yet, that I've seen. I haven't had any angry principals calling me to say that students are sharing something they shouldn't be sharing. Maybe that's because LibraryBox is low-tech enough that it hasn't risen to the attention of those folks.

The people that are using it seem to be pretty understanding of the goals and the ethos—to share information openly where it would otherwise not be shared. I've had a couple of encounters with rights holders, publishers' representatives, and so on where they've

asked how I actively prevent people from pirating their works. My response is that I don't keep people from doing anything. I've given people a tool. A hammer can build a house or commit homicide. It's not a reason to not make a hammer.

Personally, I've found librarians to be some of the least experimental people in terms of intellectual property rights. They're worried and they don't feel like they can push boundaries, even though we are totally within our legal rights to push boundaries. Lots of library directors are fairly gun-shy. Nobody wants to invite a lawsuit from a major publisher—libraries can't compete financially, so I understand. But at the same time I'm a fairly big proponent of libraries pushing on those boundaries.

How did you know if LibraryBox was working?

One of the more interesting things about LibraryBox is that unlike a website or another networked tool, I have no idea if people are using it. If somebody builds a LibraryBox, I have no idea unless they tell me. So the occasional pieces of feedback I get—an e-mail from a builder or a picture of a LibraryBox that someone has seen in the wild—it's the best. Once a month or so I get these updates. It's an amazing experience to have this thing that I started now be a project that people around the world are aware of and use. There's a nonprofit health education group in Ghana and South Africa doing nursing education with LibraryBox. So there's a LibraryBox hooked up to a solar panel outside of Accra teaching people how to be nurses—that's amazing. I never would have imagined that in a million years.

The feedback that I get is almost entirely positive. The only feedback that you might call negative is when people ask for additional features or wonder why we did things in a particular way. There are still people asking me about Library-Box and continuing to discover it, which suggests it's still working.

It seems like mobile Wi-Fi hotspots have become more common since you created LibraryBox. How do you see the relationship between hot spots and LibraryBox?
There are a couple of ways in which LibraryBox serves a different function from hot spots. First, in order for a hot spot to work you need cell connectivity. All a hot spot does is convert cell signal to Wi-Fi signal. So if there's no cell signal, the hot spot doesn't work. If you're a researcher delivering research to the Amazon, Wi-Fi hot spots aren't going to help you. So LibraryBox has a fit in those situations.

And the other reason LibraryBox is useful is that even with a Wi-Fi hot spot you have speed and bandwidth limitations. LibraryBox doesn't have either of those. It'll deliver content as quickly as Wi-Fi will allow, and there are no data caps. So if you want to give people access to an 8 GB video file, you can do that without bandwidth limitations, which you may not be able to do with a hot spot.

What resources did you have when you started? How did you build the project in its early stages?
My initial approach was, I'm going to spend a couple hundred bucks on physical hardware and then bang away at it until I see if it can do the thing I want it to do. In some cases that answer was no.

I failed a few times and had to revise my plans. And then when I had something I thought was useful, it was a matter of iterating.

The first couple of iterations weren't about adding features, they were about making it easier to build and use. If I'd added fancy features or enhanced some service piece instead of making it easier to use and build, I think it wouldn't have been as successful as it has been.

After the first few releases of the code, I had some ideas for features that would make it easier for other people [to] do other things with it. To customize the look and feel of the website that LibraryBox serves on a browser, for instance—that was something that you had to do by launching a terminal and hand-coding HTML, so a lot of librarians weren't going to do that unless I made it easier for them.

When I knew that was the next thing that had to be done, I realized I'd exceeded my ability to implement the vision. I could spend six months teaching myself how to do something or I could find someone who already knew how to do it, and pay a couple thousand dollars to get it done. So then I started thinking about fund-raising, and that's when I did the Kickstarter. I was one of the first library-focused Kickstarter projects. I needed $3,000 [to] $4,000 to buy hardware and pay developers, but the Kickstarter blew up and got much more attention than I thought it would.

What's next for you and LibraryBox? Do you want the project to grow or change in any way?
LibraryBox is an ongoing project—development is ongoing but it's slow because everyone working on it now is a volunteer. It was part of the 2016 Google

Summer of Code. [Google Summer of Code pairs university students with open-source projects to earn stipends while providing coding.] We had a student working with us on creating an iOS app for LibraryBox. Right now there's no passive findability—there's no way to know if a LibraryBox is in use nearby unless you specifically look for it. With the new app, your mobile device could alert you when you're in the presence of a LibraryBox network.

Nobody's getting rich off this. I wouldn't be still working on this four years later as a volunteer if I didn't think it deserves to exist in the world. The fact that it's helped anyone anywhere get educated is enough reason for me to keep it around.

Separately, I was one of the 2015 grantees of Knight News Challenge library awards, for another project called Measure the Future. That project is about helping libraries to better understand what happens in their spaces. Basically it's an attention metric. We use sensors and software to watch how people move through library space and create a heat map to give a clear sense of how the spaces are used. The project is strategic in terms of being able to put a sensor in an area where you want long-term understanding of the space. And it's also tactical, because you can point sensors at a book display and see how many people stop one day, then change it and see how many people stop the next day. You can do very quick A/B testing of signage changes, displays, and so on with these sensors and make short-term or long-term decisions about library space. We've been working on it for eighteen months and are just launching it now.

TACTICAL LIBRARY CASE STUDY 2:
SHELFLOGIC, AKA "THE DEWEYLESS" LIBRARY SYSTEM

IN JUNE 2007, A QUIET REBELLION TOOK PLACE IN THE PERRY BRANCH LIBRARY in Maricopa County, Arizona. The newest addition to the seventeen-branch system, the Perry library chose to break ranks with over a hundred and thirty years of library precedent and tradition. When patrons walked into the library for the first time, they were greeted with wide-open reading rooms, big windows, and low, easy-to-reach shelves. But the books weren't where they were supposed to be.

Unlike the rest of the Maricopa County library system, Perry didn't use the Dewey Decimal system. Instead, the library debuted something that was initially dubbed "Deweyless" classification, a scheme that does away with decimal numbers on spines and substitutes plain language instead. Rather than browsing the 808s or scribbling "636.70835 B587e" on a piece of scrap paper before hiking to the shelves, patrons found books labeled with words and phrases like "HEALTH FITNESS" and "NATURE ANI-MAL."

The new classification system is now known as ShelfLogic, and it's based on the shelving system used in bookstores. In the world of publishing and bookselling, books are typically classified by Book Industry Subject and Category (BISAC) headings, a scheme developed by the Book Industry Study Group (BISG). The BISAC scheme is a much simpler method for designating a book's subject than Dewey and Library of Congress. For the catalogers among us, a BISAC heading is a nine-character alphanumeric code associated with a slash-delimited descriptive phrase that summarizes what a book is about. For everyone else, the BISAC heading for a Georgette Heyer novel would be "Fiction / Romance / Historical / Regency" (and the associated BISAC code would be FIC027070).

ShelfLogic isn't exactly the same as BISAC, but it is a similarly simplified scheme that reflects a less granular and more layperson-friendly approach to classifying books than Dewey. The Maricopa Library system describes the method as "intuitive" and notes that it "relies on subject and genre to aid customers in finding . . . materials" (Maricopa County District Library, n.d.).

Why the shift? Depending on whom you ask, changing schemes was either a form of outreach to library patrons—helping them over the hurdle of the Dewey system and letting them find what they want more easily—or a concession to the "Google-ization" and general dumbing-down of culture. Some librarians applauded the move for opening up greater access to the library, while others criticized it for abandoning Dewey's rigorous architecture. Some critics feared that the system would make discovering items harder because there was no longer a specific "address" for each book on the shelf; rather, there were general subject areas that were in turn organized alphabetically.

Despite fears and criticism from librarians, it seems that the Shelf-Logic system has been popular with patrons. A month after the Perry Branch Library opened, the *Wall Street Journal* reported that "visitors have checked out about 900 items a day, far more than the 100 to 150 that typically circulate daily in nearby branches" (LaVallee 2007). And in 2013 the *Arizona Republic* asked, "Have you noticed that some shelves at South-east Regional Library in Gilbert are still bare? . . . The bare shelves are a result of the Maricopa County Library District's decision to change its classification system" (Perera 2013).

The surge in checkouts can't be attributed to ShelfLogic alone. It likely also has to do with the new branch location, the comfortable furniture and bookstore-style shelving, and the library's efforts to replace damaged and out-of-date materials with new ones. But ShelfLogic has clearly played a role and has caught the attention of several other public library systems. Shortly after Maricopa County opened the "Deweyless" Perry Branch Library, Colorado's Rangeview Library District trialed a related system it called Wordthink, labeling books with minimal category and subcategory terms. The Darien, Connecticut, public library system also reclassed its children's book collection using colors and simply worded, intuitive categories like "Learn to Read" and "Folk/Fairytale." In Illinois, librarians Joanna Kolendo and Melissa Rice were named ALA Movers and Shakers for their work taking the Frankfort Public Library District to a Deweyless system. And in New York City, librarians at the Ethical Culture Fieldston School, a private prep school, developed a Deweyless classification scheme they call Metis, for the ancient Greek Titan and goddess of wisdom.

By 2013, Maricopa County was convinced that the innovation was an improvement and subsequently converted its entire library system to ShelfLogic.

Key Principles: How It Speaks to Tactical Urbanism

Conditions and Causes

Print circulation rates have been in decline in American libraries for decades. The 2015 Public Library Data Service annual survey reflects this trend—even though the number of registered borrowers remains stable or increases, mean circulation per capita declines (Reid 2016). Participation in programs and classes is on the increase, as is device checkout, but declines in print and DVD/CD circulation aren't offset even by the increases in e-book circulation.

In other words, although libraries are still vital to their communities in many ways, the lending of physical items is diminishing in importance.

There are many reasons for this trend, but it might be simplest to say that modern libraries exist in a time of sea change. People read differently, purchase books and other content differently, and think about their communities, work, and leisure time differently than they did when Andrew Carnegie was funding his iconic library buildings across the country. Modern libraries are challenged to surf these complex social, technological, and economic changes.

At the same time, some librarians feel that despite its strengths, the Dewey Decimal Classification system isn't user-friendly—that its complexity may in fact push patrons away from finding and using library materials. Low library visit and circulation rates, they argue, might be due in part to the complex numeral-based Dewey system standing between people and books. The Dewey system, though it might be an excellent way to decide exactly where a book should live on the shelf, might not be a good wayfinding tool for non-librarians. A consultant who helped Maricopa County with the ShelfLogic project reports how survey participants responded to questions about the Dewey system: "I heard over and over 'those numbers scare me,' 'I don't understand them,' 'they make me feel stupid'" (Fister 2010).

From one point of view, the Maricopa County library system didn't have any problems to fix when it opened its new branch location—after all, the Dewey Decimal system worked well enough. From another point of view, the problem of declining library circulation and visits was clearly too big, complex, and even wicked for a single library to solve or ignore.

The Nature of the Intervention

Before they did anything, staff at the Maricopa County library system conducted surveys that told them more about how their patrons used the library. As a result of those surveys, Perry Branch manager Jennifer Miele knew that "over 75 percent of our customers stated that they go to the library to 'browse' for materials" (Fister 2010). In other words, Dewey's strength in providing a highly granular system for locating known items wasn't important to most visitors to the library, who only wanted to find a general section and browse within it. The library recognized the importance of including users in the process, *welcoming the community to take part in the project*. Without seeking community input, the librarians at Maricopa County wouldn't have been able to see past their own needs as maintainers of their library.

The new Perry Branch Library offered Maricopa County an opportunity to do something different—an opportunity the library staff chose to accept. But rather than leap blindly into the unknown, librarians at Maricopa County chose to implement the change to their classification scheme in *carefully deployed stages*. The Perry Branch location was a natural place to try something new because the library itself was brand new. There was no existing customer base to worry about alienating or disorienting—in fact, many library users probably never noticed anything odd about the scheme at all. Writing in *Public Libraries Online*, Cassidy Charles noted that "[t]he community's response to this change has been so overwhelmingly positive that the Maricopa County Library District has opened every new branch since with ShelfLogic and they are in the process of retro-converting the existing libraries' holdings to this model" (2012). Incremental changes helped everyone adjust to the new system and allowed the library to collect and respond to feedback about how well it was working.

Staging also meant that at any point along the way, librarians could have paused, reevaluated, or stopped the conversion if it wasn't working out. As it turned out, the system-wide transition was slower than expected, but not because library leadership had reservations about it. Library spokesperson Nelson Mitchell told the *Arizona Republic*, "The process is slower than anticipated because of limited staffing; we don't want to have to pass additional costs on to the town of Gilbert, so we are going a little slower than anticipated with the staff we have" (Perera 2013). Proceeding in stages helped keep the project's risk level low, an important consideration for any new venture and an especially important one for libraries, which typically use community resources to serve diverse and demanding audiences.

Strong patron input helped the library create a *local solution to a local problem* as well as to a problem that affects libraries across the country. Maricopa County didn't just take the bookselling industry's BISAC scheme and apply it to library shelves. Instead, staff used their knowledge of patron habits and needs to adapt BISAC for their specific clientele. Their approach, in turn, was adapted and tweaked by other libraries. Local solutions may require more fine-tuning than one-size-fits-all strategies, but they tend to produce better results because they respond to the needs of the specific community that uses them.

The Perry Branch Library served as a *proof of concept that was replicable*—with local tweaks—in many other libraries. Alternatives to Dewey, using natural language rather than numerals to welcome library users to the stacks, have by now been adopted by many libraries. The basic idea is a flexible one that has been repurposed in many different ways to serve different collections and users.

Following Up:
An Interview with Jeremy Reeder about ShelfLogic

I TALKED WITH Jeremy Reeder, deputy director of the Maricopa County Library District, to learn more about building browsable libraries, deciding what works locally, and learning how to jump off that ledge.

What made you shift to the ShelfLogic system? Why was it important to you?
We have a history of doing goofy things that are now accepted as mainstream in public libraries. We were early adopters of RFID, for instance. And all our libraries operate with a single customer service desk. Eight or nine years ago that was pretty revolutionary in public libraries, but now it's far more common. So the ShelfLogic project was very much in that tradition.

We had done focus groups and other studies that showed us that 95 percent of our customers were finding things via browsing. The vast majority weren't looking for a specific title. We won-

dered, what can we do to enhance that browsing? It bothered us that for people to find anything in the library, they had to go first to a computer. We wanted to retrain them to use signage instead.

Our then director, Harry Courtright, came up with this idea. We had a brand new library to try it in. The Perry Branch was literally a cornfield before we built it. So we didn't have an existing population with expectations about how things were done, and we could hire all our staff with the understanding that we were going to do this, so we didn't get any naysayers. We thought, if we can get everyone on board we can try it in this one place, a twenty-five-thousand-square-foot library. And if it fails, oh well.

What's the problem you were trying to solve?
We were trying to improve library usage by making it easier to find materials.

Partly we approached it with the new system, and partly through weeding what we had. We cut our collection in half. We now have much smaller shelving and collections. More books go out when they're not packed into rows and rows of shelving. We created more comfortable seating, and lower shelving so you could see the whole library.

Our biggest concern was, were the vendor relationships going to be sufficient? Our vendors do all our stickering and cataloging, so we were going to have to ask them to change all of that. We're large enough as a system that the vendors were willing [to] work with us on it. They also said they thought the profession was going this way anyway.

How did people respond to ShelfLogic?

On the first day I was at the door ready to introduce our customers to the new system, and they breezed right past me. They saw the gardening section and just went right to it and started browsing. We found that if you have halfway decent signage, they find things on their own.

We always hit our customers a lot with surveys, so of course we surveyed on the new system. The results were very positive, and our circulation rates went up as well.

In the professional library community, it was very controversial. I was part of a group that presented on this at ALA, among other places, and our whole message was, "this is what works for us in our system." And we never meant that everyone should do this. But we still got a lot of heat, particularly from people saying we were dumbing libraries down.

We let things run for a year at Perry Branch before we spread it into the other branches. During that time, we had staff from other branches work at this branch so they could see it wasn't the end of civilization to do this.

We didn't anticipate this, but now several other libraries have adapted what we've done. Our book vendors are also used by many other libraries, so we've had a lot of librarians call and ask how they can do this. It's been really satisfying helping them—and some of them are doing amazing things, like the Anythink library system in Colorado.

It's nice to see Deweyless systems working in different communities and libraries: rural and more urban, teeny-tiny and larger.

What resources did you have when you started out?

We had buy-in at the top, from then director of the Maricopa County Library system, Harry Courtright. That's the only way to do something like this. It's too much of a ledge to jump off without a net. We were able to adjust other resources because of that support. And we had very few hard costs because it was a new branch and we started with a clean slate.

We're on a separate county tax, so we report to a county board of supervisors rather than a library board. We let them know we wanted to try something new. It was a risk, but once our numbers came back positive, they were more concerned with getting a photo shoot scheduled than with anything else.

There is a cost associated with making a change like this, especially if you transition an existing collection. Every single book has to be touched when you transfer over. We assigned a dedicated transition team to take care of that when we included the other branches.

What are some of your takeaways from the project overall?

We've heard people say you can only do this successfully in a small library, a small space. I always point out Powell's Bookstore [in Portland, Oregon] as an example of a very similar setup in a much larger space. Powell's has very clear signage, using colors to help people find what they're looking for. So in reality you can do this in much larger spaces if you have the proper signage.

We find that our pages put books back on the shelf at a faster rate now, because they're alphabetized by title rather than author within a section. Titles are easier to read on the spine label, for both customers and pages. We also see fewer lost and missing items. The initial assumption was that we should lose less with Dewey, because the books would be more tightly organized, but the reality was that people didn't reshelve correctly. Now it's a more organic flow.

We also find that our staff can make decisions to change the ShelfLogic system as necessary. We give our vendors a list based on BISAC but with some homegrown changes, and when they have a question about where to put something, they ask us. Then staff get involved and debate where things should go. So the staff have more input into where things are shelved in the library.

I'm a firm believer that all libraries are local, and what works in St. Paul may not work in Boise. At the end of the day, ShelfLogic is an argument for listening to your customers. We're a popular materials library, with no archives or special materials. This [the ShelfLogic project] was just waiting for us to try it, because we don't have special collections—we even circulate our reference collection. So it was easy for us to try something goofy like this. If it hadn't worked, we would have phased it out, but it was a great petri dish to try it in.

What's next for ShelfLogic? Do you want the project to grow or change?

We're pretty content now that we're using ShelfLogic throughout our whole library district. But we've never perfected our signage—or at least, we're still improving it. There isn't a uniform system for the signage across all our branches, and we haven't found the perfect way to standardize it—whether we hang signs from the ceiling, use end caps, or put magnetic signage on the shelves. We've also had internal debates about pathfinders and maps.

Our customer groups are very different depending on which branch you're in. We have three libraries in seniors-only communities, which makes for interesting testing. Even senior customers aren't all alike—new seniors are different from older seniors. We have new seniors who want bike paths and older ones who want golf cart paths.

TACTICAL LIBRARY CASE STUDY 3: EVERYLIBRARY

MANY, IF NOT ALL, AMERICAN LIBRARIES FACE POLITICAL AND FUNDING CHAL- lenges regularly. Librarians are energetic self-advocates, but they face many obstacles in fighting cuts. For starters, public librarians faced with bad budget measures can't use public funds to mount campaigns in their own defense. Even professional associations like ALA are unable to spend more than 20 percent of their budget on direct political advocacy because of IRS regulations for 501(c)(3) nonprofits.

Further, because library support is typically nonpartisan and may not even correlate with library visitation and use, it can be tricky to know how and where to spend scarce marketing dollars (Online Computer Library Center 2013). How much do average American residents or elected officials know about their library? Which of its services have they used, and which have they valued most? Do they even know how the library is funded? Without knowing the answers to these types of questions, it's hard for librarians to know how to mount an organized, effective advocacy campaign—if they have the time, resources, and skills to do so.

For all these reasons, when local libraries go up against powerful conservative political action committees like Americans for Prosperity (backed by David and Charles Koch), funding for public libraries can seem like a lost cause. But in late 2012, an ALA staffer named John Chrastka leaped into the gap between libraries and their funding streams by creating a library-focused political action committee, otherwise known as a PAC.

EveryLibrary is a 501(c)(4) organization, with a charter "to promote public, school, and college libraries, including by advocating in support of public funding for libraries and building public awareness of public funding initiatives" (EveryLibrary.org, n.d.d). EveryLibrary works both strategically and tactically to help librarians of all types across the country defend and increase their funding sources. In an interview with *American Libraries*, Chrastka said,

> I was inspired by a PAC from outside the library world called the Conservation Campaign. Since 1996, it has acted as a 501(c)(4) to help local communities do voter education and fundraising for land use,

open spaces, and parkland ballot issues. The Conservation Campaign has, by its own account, helped local communities secure $2 billion in funding through bonds and taxes at the ballot box. (Goldberg 2012)

Under Chrastka's leadership, EveryLibrary began raising funds for libraries in need of advocacy support. In 2013 the organization supported seven local library campaigns in states from Oregon to Louisiana, winning four of them. EveryLibrary offered libraries everything from money for phone banking to consultation on library messaging, opposition research, and in-person training on getting out the vote. In addition, EveryLibrary makes campaign tools such as yard signs and phone scripts freely available to all libraries online.

One of EveryLibrary's most dramatic campaigns took place in November 2013 in Lafourche Parish, Louisiana, when Parish Council Chair Lindel Toups proposed a special Saturday election that would redirect library funds to build a new jail. The *Times*, a local newspaper, reported,

> "They're teaching Mexicans how to speak English," the council chairman said in reference to Biblioteca Hispana, a Hispanic-language segment of the Golden Meadow library branch. "Let that son of a bitch go back to Mexico. There's just so many things they're doing that I don't agree with. . . . Them junkies and hippies and food stamps [recipients] and all, they use the library to look at drugs and food stamps [on the Internet]. I see them do it." (Besson 2013)

EveryLibrary mobilized quickly, working with the local library community to call for donations and create a social media campaign in support of the library. Raising over $1,000 in twenty-four hours, the organization placed eight ads in the Lafourche area and gained widespread attention for the cause. Popular author Neil Gaiman Tweeted in support of the campaign, and media outlets from the *Los Angeles Times* to the *Huffington Post* carried the story. Despite only 15 percent of parish voters turning out, the election was a win for the library.

As of 2016, EveryLibrary had supported thirty-six library campaigns, with twenty-seven wins and over $100 million in protected or increased revenue. The organization's activities have grown to include a Rapid Response Fund to fund social media ads assisting libraries in immediate financial crisis, a conference speakers program, and even an Artist in Residence program. (The Artist in Residence program's goals are to "transform libraries from the inside out with magical thinking" and to "ignite a sense of wonder among library workers everywhere, encouraging libraries to approach with new eyes their vital role in the public sphere and the wider ecosystem of cultural institutions" [EveryLibrary.org, n.d.a].)

In August 2016 educational publishing company Gale began providing its Analytics on Demand (AOD) service to EveryLibrary in order to improve how the organization collects and analyzes library data. AOD combines anonymized ILS data with consumer demographic data to create reports on library trends. EveryLibrary plans to use AOD to refine its campaigns and produce the most bang for its buck.

Key Principles: How It Speaks to Tactical Urbanism

Conditions and Causes

Libraries operate in an increasingly politicized world—that is, a world in which politics and money are increasingly intertwined and in which there are ever more professional players in the political sphere. Even on local ballots, the stakes are high. Millions of dollars are up for grabs, and librarians must be canny and proactive about pursuing them.

But few library schools teach courses in city, district, county, or state voting laws. Few librarians have experience getting out the vote, or creating awareness campaigns, or forging partnerships with local ballot committees or advocacy groups. Fewer still have the skills to create a marketing plan for their library. And probably almost none have experience going up against hardball politicos like the Koch brothers or loose cannons like Council Chair Lindel Toups. It's hard to blame librarians for this—after all, they trained to be librarians, not politicians. And there are those pesky statutes that keep libraries from using tax money to tell voters exactly what to do.

Librarians face a complex and potentially wicked set of problems in what John Chrastka calls "the advocacy gap" in "political action and electioneering" (Chrastka 2013). Going door to door, talking to voters in the right way and about the right things, forming key partnerships—all these things take political savvy and know-how that can be overwhelming for librarians who just want to do the jobs they trained for. Gauging and affecting public opinion are famously hard to do, especially where people's wallets are concerned. And even when there's a clear way to measure success—a yes or no on a ballot measure—the work required to get there is complex, time-consuming, and specialized.

The Nature of the Intervention

EveryLibrary is an interesting example of a tactical library intervention because it's also a great example of strategic planning and action. That is, EveryLibrary's charter is focused on high-level, organized planning with long-term goals. But as we saw at the start of this book, the best tactics operate in service to strategy, and no strategy can accomplish much without the tactics to support it. EveryLibrary is focused not only on planning but on action, and it uses a tactical approach to help it accomplish its long-term strategic goals.

One tactic that EveryLibrary has used successfully is *starting small and growing over time*. The organization was established in late 2012. In 2013 the organization's goal was to support at least five library ballot committees—a goal that it beat by supporting seven library campaigns with its initial donations (EveryLibrary.org, n.d.b). By 2016 EveryLibrary had added multiple board members and advisors, won many more library campaigns, launched new programs, and won in-kind support from Gale. By carefully staging its growth, EveryLibrary scaled its ambitions to fit its abilities, avoided spreading itself too thin, and successfully built its political capital.

Although EveryLibrary is a national nonprofit, its work is closely tied to *local issues and local solutions*. EveryLibrary contributes a big-picture understanding of politics but works in service to local ballot committees. This approach is particularly important in the political arena, where locals are likely to resent the intrusion of outsiders and perceived special interests. As Chrastka commented to *American Libraries*,

In every case, we will not be coming into a district independent of the local library committee. We will, however, not be shy about talking to local government about how libraries build communities and change lives; about how librarians are partners for local businesses, educators, and parents; and how, as a country, we are better off when a local community has a library with the right funding, staffing, and collections. (Goldberg 2012)

EveryLibrary's charter is built around advocacy and awareness, but it implicitly includes education and empowerment. Almost all the organization's programs are explicitly structured to develop library advocacy expertise across the country. "We will not help you twice," the organization warns on the web page describing its Rapid Response Fund for libraries in crisis: "You will learn how to build an actionable network of your own" (EveryLibrary.org, n.d.c). EveryLibrary's goal is a *decentralized, populist membership* able to advocate for itself. And the grassroots response shows that librarians are willing to pitch in: a 2014 *Library Journal* article noted, "In its first year, EveryLibrary raised more than $35,000, about half from hundreds of individual donors" ("Leader of the PAC" 2014).

With all this on its plate, it's admirable that EveryLibrary still finds the time to add a little *humor and delight* to its offerings. The Artist in Residence program is both functional and whimsical, serving to improve and deepen the public's understanding of libraries while also intriguing—or maybe perplexing—the average voter who considers the library nothing more than a building full of books. Steve Kemple, who served as the organization's first Artist in Residence in 2015, spent his time curating art installations and performances in libraries and encouraging library staff and patrons across the country to participate in organized activities such as high-fiving each other whenever the International Space Station passed overhead. Whether voters find this kind of intervention charming or annoying, it shows that libraries aren't just about books and ballots, and it adds another human dimension to the organization.

Following Up: An Interview with John Chrastka, Executive Director of EveryLibrary

I TALKED WITH EveryLibrary founder John Chrastka to learn more about pursuing library political advocacy, knowing how to talk to voters, and getting "bigger than librarians."

Tell me about how EveryLibrary got started.

Someone once told me that it's the first new idea since Dewey died. Dewey set up NYLA, the New York Library Association, and that library association model has been in place for a hundred and forty or a hundred and sixty years. It works great for 364 days of advocacy, but it breaks down on election day because of legal constraints on 501(c)(3)s. The IRS caps direct lobbying by 501(c)(3)s at a very low level—20 percent of their overall activities.

EveryLibrary is a 501(c)(4), a political action committee, so it's free of those constraints. It's also a start-up—and as a start-up, you have to be first, best, or unique. We're all three. We deploy our ideas in a rapidly iterative way. What we've learned is, we have to understand the rest of the library ecosystem so we can find our niche in it.

How would you describe the problem you're trying to solve?

We were trying to find a way within the IRS caps on how much library associations can lobby for library issues. Those caps, by the way, apply not just to lobbying to elected officials but also on lobbying to voters, because the voter is considered the same as a member of

Congress when they're reviewing a ballot measure. They're going to enact or not enact a measure based on their decision.

We were also attempting to teach librarians to be politically literate. We want librarians to start realizing their own power and learning how to move that power into an active voice. We train libraries to do door-to-door library card sign-up campaigns and survey work. In other words, we teach librarians to radically violate the distance between them and their public by jumping over the reference desk.

You lead in two ways—out of your strength and out of your humility. Strength alone is megalomaniacal. Humility alone is sycophantic. Librarians are really good at being humble. We want to teach librarians that they have strength and power, to help them realize their leadership potential.

What resources did you have when you started out?

We started with zero dollars. We knew we had to be validated by the library industry, by our base, if we were going to do this. So in September of 2012 we put out a call saying that we have zero dollars and an idea, challenging the library community to raise $50,000 between Labor Day and Election Day. If we succeeded, we felt that would validate our ideas and also let us work on our first campaign. We raised $42,000, all from individual donors.

We're a PAC so we don't have to disclose our donors, but we are as transparent as possible within the law. We publish our Guidestar profile because we believe in the transparency of money in politics. We ask our donors to self-disclose and 97 percent do. The ones that don't—I think they just miss the box asking them to identify themselves. We exist because of Citizens United even though we think Citizens United is a bad idea.

We give money to almost every single ballot campaign committee that we support. We were finally able to pay ourselves in year four of our existence.

Having an Artist in Residence is pretty unusual for a PAC. Why did you choose to do that?

The Artist in Residence program was intended to add delight and creativity to our mission. If you can't have a discussion about ideas that includes the arts then all you're doing is making logic models and writing position papers and strategy documents. You have to have both—delight and logic—to leaven the conversation properly. There's also a truth about the exercise of politics, which is that it's not just policy. It's creative and generative.

The residency program will be repeated in odd-numbered years, because even-numbered years have too many elections. I'd love to have a dancer in that position.

What do you want EveryLibrary to accomplish?

We're looking to supplement, not to supplant. At the same time, we know we're disruptive to the library ecosystem because we're establishing a new niche. There aren't enough resources in the

ecosystem to sustain another niche, so we need to grow bigger in one way or another.

Our key driver for our first five or six years is to get bigger than only librarians as supporters. By that I mean, we need to build new coalitions with people who aren't like librarians—people who don't share all the same characteristics and opinions as librarians. For instance, we can actually talk to the Tea Party people about prosperity, economic liberty, and choice—all values that are right in our wheelhouse and in theirs too. We've got to start talking to people who are suspicious about how their tax dollars are spent, but still in line with some of our shared values.

We're attempting to disrupt the image of the uncaring library nonuser. We have an emotional perception that, if you don't come to my library, then you don't like me. That's not true at all. There are people who like and love the library, there are people who are rationally ignorant but favorably disposed toward it, people who are perfectly capable of providing support in terms of their time or money. We need to understand and reach them.

Our big goal is to become like the NRA [National Rifle Association] or Sierra Club for libraries. We want to be a national-level, nationally recognized political advocacy organization for libraries. To do that we need to build in two ways. One is in resources for the organization—we need more people and more money. And the other is to shift our approach to advocacy from reactive to proactive. We can't sustain a national movement on a retrenching, reactive "save our libraries" message.

TACTICAL LIBRARY CASE STUDY 4:
BOSTON STREET LAB'S STOREFRONT LIBRARY

IN 1956 THE CITY OF BOSTON APPROVED THE DEMOLITION OF A READING ROOM and former branch of the Boston Public Library at 130 Tyler Street, in the Chinatown neighborhood. The building was destroyed to make way for an elevated portion of the city's Central Artery, which today provides passage through the city for Interstate 93, U.S. Route 1, and Massachusetts Route 3. Ironically, the Artery's route was later shifted, but by that time the library was already gone (Fox 2012).

Sixty years later, despite public petitions and demonstrations and the persistent efforts of the Friends of the Chinatown Library, the neighborhood still lacks a library (Lowery 2014). It is one of the few areas of the city without a place for residents to borrow books, use the Internet, or attend job training or reading programs. There are no municipal funds earmarked to build a new library and no clear path to getting them.

In late 2009 Boston newcomers Sam and Leslie Davol added their voices to the chorus demanding a new Chinatown library—but they did it in an unusual way. Rather than petition city councillors again, the couple installed what they called the Chinatown Storefront Library in a three-thousand-square-foot vacant storefront at 640 Washington Street. With space donated by a real estate development company, architectural consulting from students at Harvard's Graduate School of Design, and more than five thousand Chinese- and English-language books from the Boston Public Library, the Storefront Library was a joint venture in recognition of a long-standing need. The Storefront Library also offered public computers with Internet access as well as volunteer staff who provided reading programs for kids, translation assistance, and programs such as English conversation groups.

All this was available to Chinatown residents from October 2009 until February 2010—just under five months. Then the Storefront Library closed, the books were removed, and the space was rented out to another tenant. Although this venture might seem like a failure, Sam and Leslie Davol don't believe it was. In their opinion, their organization—Boston Street Lab—stepped into an ongoing, long-term effort by the Friends of the Chinatown Library to secure a permanent library for the neighborhood. With the Friends' approval and cooperation, they tried a different approach to the pitch:

> The purpose of the project was to give people the experience of a library, as well as model lighter and quicker ways of realizing needs for civic, cultural and community space. It was agreed that the installation would be temporary so that Boston Street Lab could borrow space and realize it quickly and inexpensively, and so that the Friends of the Chinatown Library could continue their campaign for a permanent branch of the Boston Public Library following the project. (Street Lab, n.d.)

Although they can't claim immediate, complete, and concrete success—there's still no Chinatown branch of the Boston Public Library—the Davols point to a number of accomplishments from the project. "The Storefront Library successfully gave people—particularly children—the experience of a library in Chinatown. It also provided much-needed public space and increased the capacity of a variety of other nonprofit organizations to engage the public at street level and coordinate their work" (Street Lab, n.d.). The project garnered lots of media attention as well as the notice and support of city and government officials. Boston's mayor attended the Storefront Library opening. The governor awarded the project a special citation for community service. And the Chinese Progressive Association, a long-standing community empowerment organization, recognized Boston Street Lab with its Social Justice and Innovation Award.

The fight for a permanent Chinatown library benefited from the Storefront Library project too. The media attention helped drive interest in the long-term struggle, bringing new members and new funding opportunities to help the Friends of the Chinatown Library in its work. In 2012 the Asian Community Development Corporation opened a small storefront library called the Chinatown Lantern, modeling it closely on the Boston Street Lab project (Fox 2012). The Chinatown Lantern included a temporary reading room, which provided books, English-language and computer literacy classes, and children's programs for ten months.

And the Storefront Library project has caused ripples far beyond the Chinatown neighborhood or the city. It helped popularize the idea of pop-up libraries, temporary service points that appear in areas of high need to energize the community and highlight the demand. The Davols point to pop-up and storefront libraries in Allentown, Pennsylvania, Evanston, Illinois, and even Cairo, Egypt, that either directly credit the Boston Street Lab project for their inspiration or demonstrate the same concepts (Street Lab, n.d.)

Key Principles: How It Speaks to Tactical Urbanism

Conditions and Causes

The residents of Boston's Chinatown neighborhood have clearly shown what they need and want—a permanent, well-resourced branch of their city's public library system. The reasons for that lack are as complex as they are in the South Bronx—money, history, culture, and infrastructure all play a part. Mimi Fong, an activist involved in the struggle, told Boston .com that the Boston Public Library had been supportive of the effort to open a new branch but that its own resources were limited. "They have their own financial constraints, needless to say. . . . And we absolutely understand that" (Fox 2012).

Regardless of the difficulty of launching a new branch library, it's clearly a problem when citizens and taxpayers aren't given equitable access to shared resources such as a city library system. Like food deserts—urban areas without centrally located groceries or markets to buy reasonably priced, good-quality food—so-called book deserts are a hallmark of a neglected, underserved neighborhood. And the problem has serious, even wicked ramifications. As Alia Wong points out in a 2016 *Atlantic* article, book deserts lead to "word gaps" (differences in vocabulary between kids who grow up surrounded by books and conversation and those who don't) and gaps in later educational attainment (Wong 2016).

Activists with the Friends of the Chinatown Library have struggled for years to win basic resources in the face of a system that is too underfunded, too indifferent, or too mismanaged to offer what residents need. Everyone agrees that the lack of a public library branch in the neighborhood is a singular, detrimental omission—but so far, that agreement hasn't translated into a solution to the problem.

The Nature of the Intervention

The Storefront Library is perhaps one of our more challenging examples of a tactical library intervention. Was it successful, or did it fail? It would be satisfying to see that the city of Boston had found some new, creative way to fund a Chinatown branch library after seeing the popularity and success of the Storefront Library installation. But that's not the case. When our underlying problems prove harder to solve than we'd like, what other kinds of success can we celebrate? What encouragement can we give ourselves to keep trying new, ingenious, collaborative engagements with the problem?

The fight to secure permanent, big-ticket resources—to build, staff, and maintain a new neighborhood library, for instance—is grueling and costly. It's also important. Everyone involved in the Storefront Library project agreed that the goal was still a permanent branch of the Boston Public Library in the Chinatown neighborhood. But staging the Storefront Library as a *short-term, temporary* project offered a way around those big-money obstacles. Securing a space, collection, and volunteer staff was much simpler to do for a four-month project with a clearly defined sunset than it has proved to be for a permanent library branch.

The Storefront Library served as a clear *proof of concept* for the permanent library that the neighborhood needs by successfully offering many of the services that such a facility would provide. If there was any doubt in the minds of city or Boston Public Library officials that the Chinatown neighborhood would adopt and use a library—if there was doubt, in other words, that it would be worth the investment—that doubt was strongly challenged by the success of the Storefront Library. Not only was the library busy and popular but it attracted fruitful partnerships from corporations, agencies, and individuals as well as attention from the media and imitation in other locations.

Sam and Leslie Davol placed *explicit value on the intangible outcomes* of the Storefront Library project. Rather than seeking to address the neighborhood's need head-on by supplying it with exactly what it needed—a permanent branch of the public library system—they chose to demon-strate the goodwill, partnerships, opportunities, and social capital that they could generate with their work. Tactically speaking, these intangibles are highly valuable assets that can be leveraged to forward the long-term quest for a permanent library building.

The Davols recognized the need for a *local solution to a local problem.* They were residents of the neighborhood, meaning their intervention was both self-interested and rooted in genuine understanding of the issues in play. However, as relatively recent white transplants to a historically Asian neighborhood with a history of fighting its own battles, their role was far from simple. Rather than steamroll or ignore the existing advocacy effort, they sought (and received) the blessing of the Friends of Chinatown Library group and agreed on an approach that would help promote that group's long-term efforts.

TACTICAL ILS CASE STUDY 5:
KOIOS, MARCEDIT, AND ACCESS CHECKER

OUR FIFTH LIBRARY CASE STUDY IS A BUNDLE OF THREE SEPARATE PROJECTS, each of them related to the ILS. The ILS—integrated library system, for any nonlibrarians who've made it this far—is the backbone of the modern library. It's the software that librarians use to keep track of items in the col-lection and to display them to the public through the online catalog. It's also the system we use to track patron information, fines, order and purchasing records, and much more. The ILS is all-powerful and all-important.

It's also, unfortunately, usually a complex and demanding product that requires a lot of care and feeding by library staff. When things go wrong with the ILS, it's not always quick or easy to get fixes from the software vendor—often, librarians find they must create their own solutions. This case study bundles three examples of tactical approaches to improving the ILS.

The first example, Koios, is perhaps the newest of the three. Koios addresses this problem: although libraries champion free access to information, our collections are usually hidden from Internet searches. A casual Google search on the title of a book will produce Amazon results at the top of the list while library catalog results either won't show up at all or will be ranked so low that few searchers will find them. Most web searchers don't think to go directly to library websites to try the catalog for something they'd like to read, watch, or hear. And if they do go, they often balk at using the library catalog, which isn't as intuitive as Google. As Koios's team puts it on their Knight Foundation News Challenge funding pitch page, "Library non-users often have the same two objections to using the library: they don't know what's available to them, and they think it takes too long" (Gordner 2016).

Koios CEO and founder Trey Gordner attempts to solve this problem with a free browser extension that notifies patrons when they search for an item owned by their local library. Users download a free plug-in for Chrome, Firefox, or Safari and set up their preferences to indicate their local library and nearest branch. An Amazon search will then produce a pop-up window that alerts users if the item they're searching for is owned by the library and gives them a link to request it. Libraries pay a fee to have their collections included in the Koios database and reflected in the browser tool. The Koios start-up team chose Amazon as its initial test case but is projected to expand service into Netflix, IMDB, Wikipedia, and other common online media providers.

The second project, MarcEdit, has been around since 1999 when Oregon State University librarians were presented with a large batch of MARC catalog records in need of editing. Over forty-five thousand records needed work to ensure that the public catalog accurately represented what the library owned, but there were no tools up to doing the job. The scenario is familiar to many technical services librarians. As David Cook wrote in *Feliciter*, "What happens when someone identifies problems in metadata records? What happens if those twenty thousand new articles were actually catalogued as videos by mistake? . . . More often than not the data remains problematic, as we don't have the money or the time to handle it" (2014, 24). Many libraries pay vendors or contractors to correct MARC records, which can cost thousands of dollars.

Fortunately for Oregon State, library staffer Terry Reese had the skills and the initiative to craft his own editing program, which he dubbed MarcEdit. Initially, Reese saw the project as a one-off fix to an immediate need. "Working entirely on my own, by the light of my small computer lamp in my den, I hacked out the code for the application" (Reese 2013a). Later, he recognized the value of the tool for other projects and other users. He was convinced to invest the effort to create a graphical user interface (GUI) to make the program easier for nonprogrammer librarians to use. Thousands of library staff have since downloaded MarcEdit to quickly and easily edit batches of MARC records on Windows, Mac, and Linux.

The third project addresses yet another problem with the ILS—making sure that libraries get what they pay for. E-resources cataloger Kristina Spurgin at the University of North Carolina at Chapel Hill was familiar with handling the library's purchases of large digital packages of e-books and streaming media. However, she noticed that there was no practical way for library staff to make sure that all the licensed content was accessible to users through the online catalog or that the included MARC records accurately reflected what was purchased. Most often, the only way libraries found out that supposedly available content wasn't there was when patrons encountered a 404 or "no access" error and informed the library. With some packages including tens or even hundreds of thousands of titles, there was no good way for librarians to manually check every link, and most link-checking software wasn't capable of distinguishing between correct access and error messages on vendor landing pages.

Spurgin happened to be teaching herself the programming language Ruby at the time she considered this problem, and she used that skill to create a tool she called Access Checker. Although Access Checker can't be used to verify access to electronic journal articles, it can check for correct access to e-books collections from common providers such as Wiley, Springer, and SAGE or to streaming media from vendors such as Alexander Street Press and Kanopy. The tool is able to distinguish between a "no access" page and full access to the titles that the library should have, and when it's configured correctly it can check thousands of pages automatically without triggering the alarms vendors put in place to discourage mass downloading. Spurgin's tool is command-line rather than GUI-based, making it harder for noncoding librarians to adopt, but she has shared it freely on the popular developer site GitHub and welcomes improvements from other library programmer-developers.

Key Principles: How It Speaks to Tactical Urbanism

Conditions and Causes

All three of these projects address technical challenges associated with how the ILS represents the library's collection to its users and its own staff. In an ideal world, the enterprise software systems that librarians buy or license from ILS vendors would be problem-free and would always reflect the library's holdings fully, accurately, and simply. Digital records would be error-free and compatible across platforms. All the electronic databases, streaming media services, and digital repositories that libraries pay for and maintain would fit neatly together like puzzle pieces, resulting in a single user-friendly interface for library users to find everything they need from a simple Internet search.

The reality, obviously, is very different. Librarians must constantly check, doctor, and maintain the records and platforms that connect users with the print and digital collection. In many cases (as Spurgin's Access Checker tool reveals) there is no reliable way even to know when a problem arises, or to fix it before it creates an obstacle to access. In other cases (as Reese's MarcEdit project shows) there is no commercially available tool that can fix known problems—or the available tools aren't up to the task or aren't cost-effective. Because of the vast size and diversity of modern library collections, and the complexity of their digital records, librarians must constantly build creative ways to corral unruly but essential data.

In addition, Koios and related tools such as LibX shows that there's a human element to the ILS challenge. User habits and expectations are changing—people no longer consider the library to be the first or only source of information. Instead, they do simple Google searches for what they want to find. If the library doesn't emerge quickly and easily near the top of those search results, it might as well not exist. Gordner, who is not a librarian but a business major, recognizes the importance of meeting library users and nonusers where they are—in Amazon, Netflix, and Google. It doesn't matter how correct and complete our ILS records are if nobody's visiting the library website and we're not reaching out beyond its confines.

The Nature of the Intervention

Given limited resources, all three of these projects adopted the classic tactic of *starting small*. Koios didn't spend years developing a one-size-fits-all tool that would expose every library's collection to Internet searchers—that would have taken time and money that the start-up didn't have. Instead, developers identified the library's top competitor in Internet book searching—Amazon—and started there. Proving that the tool worked in the most relevant context helped make the case to future funders and library clients that it could and should be expanded farther. Terry Reese and Kristina Spurgin developed their tools solo—and Reese actually considered retiring his after he finished the project he designed it for. Both MarcEdit and Access Checker began life as simple coding projects in response to an immediate need. Only later did they become more versatile, user-friendly, and widely adopted. Starting small gave all three projects room to learn, experiment, and respond to feedback without losing much time, money, or ground.

Both Reese and Spurgin developed their tools in part as *passion projects*—that is, they were motivated not only by the need to fix a problem but also by excitement, curiosity, and enjoyment. Reese writes, "MarcEdit gives me an opportunity to work on things that I'm passionate about . . . it scratches an itch" (2013b). Spurgin notes that Access Checker was one of her first coding projects, undertaken as she was teaching herself Ruby. Although both Reese and Spurgin were charged in their positions with managing aspects of the ILS and solving technical problems, neither of them was specifically directed to build the tools they did. Personal enthusiasm played a major role in both projects, motivating Reese and Spurgin to go above and beyond the tools they already had at hand.

To different extents, all three of these projects represent *local solutions to local problems*. Although libraries usually rely on software vendors to develop and provide ILSs, there's a limit to the support that most vendors provide. Everyday workflow problems, such as glitchy MARC records, and bigger zeitgeist problems, such as users failing to directly search library catalogs, are often outside the scope of what vendors can fix, even if libraries have the budgets to pay them. Instead of looking outward for solutions to these problems, all three projects turned to the expertise of librarians themselves. Reese and Spurgin provided their own and supplemented it with the advice and encouragement of colleagues and (eventually) the library developer community. Trey Gordner formed a team of coders, librarians, and library school students and faculty, then beta-tested Koios with several library systems before taking it public. As any collection management or cataloging librarian will confirm, the ILS use case is different from any other. Developing tools for the ILS context requires intimate understanding of and experience with its specific challenges.

Access Checker is open-source software, meaning anyone is welcome to edit it. MarcEdit is closed (only Terry Reese can edit the code), but it's freely available for other librarians to use, and because it's easy and effective, it has developed a broad user base. Both tools have a *broad base of decentralized ownership*, with librarians either contributing code or providing feedback and answering each other's questions. This approach distributes responsibility for improvements throughout the community, leveraging the passion and enthusiasm of many librarians, lowering investment risk for everyone, and helping the tools improve beyond the limited resources of any individual user. Although Koios has pursued a start-up business model rather than an open-source sharing one, Gordner's team has sought the input of several library systems and librarian advisors to develop the tool.

Following Up: An Interview with Terry Reese, Creator of MarcEdit

I TALKED TO Terry Reese, head of digital initiatives at Ohio State University Library, about dealing with the joys and pains of a large user community, giving catalogers the tools they need, and coping with pages and pages (and pages) of spreadsheets.

What made you create MarcEdit? What problem were you trying to solve?
I was a student worker at the University of Oregon. I had a computer science background and was working in libraries to help to pay for college. In the Map Library we were cataloging historical maps, so I started building some tools that would later be used in MarcEdit to learn more about MARC.

MarcEdit didn't take shape, however, until I was at Oregon State University [OSU] and the cataloging department was in the midst of a large data clean-up project. Over a number of years, SuDoc numbers had been flipped to incorrect LC call numbers, and this was impacting access. There were notebooks with pages and pages of spreadsheets printed out, and the idea was that everybody was going to pick some pages and fix them by hand. The project was expected to take years to manually go into each record and fix all the call numbers. I told Kyle Banerjee, an OSU librarian, that I'd been working on a coding project that might be able to help if he could give me a delimited file of the spreadsheet and the MARC records. It took ten minutes to fix the problem using a script and the tools I had.

How did the MarcEdit project grow over time?
After completing the project, Kyle suggested that I make this available to other people. But as a nonlibrarian at the time, I had no means to put my work out more broadly. Kyle advocated for and worked to get me participating in regional conferences to talk about the project. That helped me learn what the issues were at other nearby libraries. The real turning point was getting a community built around the program.

It took a while for me to get out of Oregon and start talking about it more broadly. I saw people discuss it on lists and answered their questions online, but Kyle was the one who talked it up the most.

How did people respond to MarcEdit once you brought it out more widely?
Around 2000, most metadata batch editing was being done in library systems departments, not by technical services staff because the tools available to do this work were largely developed for programmers. MarcEdit pushed the ability to do batch edits back into technical services because staff didn't have to know how to program to do it. So technical services people got really interested.

This was also a time when a lot of libraries started focusing more on electronic resources. There were a lot more e-books and e-journals in our collections. Managing metadata for these materials was very time-consuming. No one had the time to do it, but technical services librarians wanted to do it, they just needed the right tool for the job.

MarcEdit isn't open-source software. How has the user community contributed to the tool?

Providing user support was the hardest part of the project. That's the part that could have killed it because there's just so much need. The willingness of others in the community to answer questions and give workshops and talk about it in their work has helped keep it going. I give maybe two workshops a year now. The MarcEdit community really supports it.

There's a MarcEdit discussion list run by George Mason University. Before the list, I would deal with hundreds of questions over e-mail. Now the list takes care of a lot of those. There are about 1,800 people on it, and the list is archived.

Some folks have been using MarcEdit for a very, very long time. You can still go to ALA conference sessions on MarcEdit. There are a couple at Midwinter Meeting this year that I wish I could drop in on.

What do you know about the MarcEdit user community?

There's an auto-update feature people can opt into using that checks for a new version of the program every time it is used. If people are updating, they're still actively using the tool and it's worth my continuing to support it. It also gives me an idea of where users are geographically and what operating systems they're using. I'm trying to stop supporting Windows XP, but there's a large population of users in the developing world still using it.

There are about twenty thousand active users of MarcEdit now. Of that core group of users, it's about a sixty-forty split between North American users and users in the rest of the world. Outside of Antarctica, Greenland, and maybe North Korea, there are very few parts of the world where there's not a MarcEdit user.

Are there any downsides to having such a big user community?

There was a time when this was a hobby project. I did it because it was fun and I could do whatever I wanted. But when it grew in popularity, I had to think about it differently. I couldn't just add or take things away. That would be too disruptive for the users. Change tends to happen a little slower as some changes need to be incremental due to impacts they will have on workflows. So now I use plug-ins to try out things that not everybody has to put into application.

Once people start using a tool and organizations bless it, you can't break it or take it away. Of course that's partly because you'd impact the users, but there's also potentially someone who vouched for it and has staked some organizational capital on it, and you'd be hurting that individual and the institution if you took it away. There would also be a lot of people upset at you, which isn't good.

People ask me for advice on starting a project like this and I tell them, you're going to have to spend three to four years working on it alone, best case scenario, even if you make it open-source. The first group you build isn't a developers' group, it's a group of supporters. The development part is relatively easy—there are technical problems to solve, but building the community is much harder.

It's hard to pivot quickly when you have to bring a lot of people along. It takes me years to change a major version number, because it involves a lot of pain for individuals and it's painful for me too. For instance, if a government agency uses your tool, they have to vet you whenever it updates. I get phone calls from government agencies when I change version numbers.

Why was MarcEdit important to you? Why spend so much time and energy on a project like this, without a direct financial return?
Around 2004 or 2005 I had opportunities to monetize the tool. But I didn't go into libraries to make money, apparently. It wasn't something I was ever really tempted to do. And now that it's been out for a while I wouldn't.

Every now and then I kick around the idea of making MarcEdit open-source. I haven't done it yet, and at first that was because it was still mostly written in Assembly and I didn't think there were many library developers who could or would work on it in that language. Now it's in C#, so there's a broader community that could modify it. But I'm not a cataloger anymore and I work on this in my spare time. I honestly worry that if I had a lot more people contributing to the project, I couldn't keep up with the issues and maintain it anymore. And I still enjoy working on the tool and with the community too much to let it go.

What's next for MarcEdit?
I keep a list of enhancements that people suggest. In the development process, I keep in mind that MarcEdit is just one of many tools you'll use if you're a metadata person. I try to work closely with people who build those other tools and create ways for MarcEdit to work directly with them or facilitate the process of moving data into and out of them easily.

I work a lot with OCLC's API [application program interface], and I work with libraries that use Alma because there's an API for it and people can use MarcEdit to edit records that way. I work with OpenRefine and the linked data community—moving MARC records into OpenRefine is a pain, so now MarcEdit has a tool that facilitates that. I also support formats like JSON because they're useful in other contexts.

The community asked for a Mac version of MarcEdit for a long time. I'm not a big fan of Mac systems, and I had no intention of buying a Mac to do this kind of development. So Whitni Watkins and Francis Kayiwa got together to prove there was interest and crowdsourced me a Mac. And they did it, so I ported the program. I spent a year and a half porting the program from C# to Object C.

I'm also working on figuring out how MarcEdit fits into the semantic web. BIBFRAME, for instance—whether or not we go that route, the concepts will be useful. The intermediary step of taking string data in MARC and reconciling it into objects isn't easy.

Part of the work I do with the Program for Cooperative Cataloging at the Library of Congress is figuring out how to provide a platform to do this kind of work systematically and as a part of production work. That's been interesting because a lot of that work is me talking to individual providers about how their services can be more responsive.

5

LIBRARY MEETS CITY

S WE'VE ALREADY SEEN, SOMETIMES A LIBRARY IS VERY LIKE a city. And that's not just a metaphor—whether your library is academic, public, school, or something else, it's part of a larger social and civic structure. Public libraries offer community programs such as computer skills training, job search preparation, and early childhood literacy that benefit their towns and cities in very concrete ways. School libraries help get kids on track to do better in school throughout their lives and offer stable places to learn and engage in after-school activities that lighten the load on working parents. Academic libraries help produce an informed citizenry and help graduate educated and employable students who can boost the local, regional, and national economies. Wise city governments recognize the vast civic benefits of a healthy library system, both financially and culturally.

In this chapter we'll explore some tactical interventions that straddle the line between the worlds of the city and the library, showing how the right kind of tactical intervention in libraries can have a ripple effect that spreads far out into the community.

LIBRARY MEETS CITY CASE STUDY 1:
STORY POD AND MAGDEBURG OPEN AIR LIBRARY

MAGDEBURG IS A VENERABLE GERMAN CITY THAT HAS SEEN CENTURIES OF change, from its medieval origins through two devastating world wars, more than fifty years of Communist occupation, and the postwar reunification of the country. These days it's both an industrial and postindustrial town, home to manufacturing and shipping businesses as well as high vacancy and unemployment rates. The economy continues to struggle, and when Magdeburg's district (public) library was demolished, no funds were available to rebuild it.

Toronto has had its own ups and downs, but in 2016 it was Canada's largest city, with over two and a half million people living and working in just under four hundred square miles. Like hundreds of others, the small neighboring town of Newmarket has been absorbed into the Greater Toronto Area and become a bedroom community. Newmarket has a public library system and a prospering mall, but the city council sought an innovative way to enliven its public spaces and encourage its residents to gather in the historic downtown area as well as to make Newmarket an attractive destination for day trips from the city.

Although Magdeburg and Newmarket are very different cities, they've adopted a similar solution to their challenges: the design and installation of an architecturally interesting communal book exchange space that's freely open to the public. Instead of housing a permanent collection, the book spaces welcome members of the public to contribute their own reading materials, similar to the Little Free Library model but on a grand scale.

In 2005 in Magdeburg, city officials and architects began working with local residents to construct a proof-of-concept design near the former library's vacant lot. They used beer crates to fabricate a full-size temporary replica of the building they proposed, creating a kind of dumbbell footprint with a covered dogtrot connecting two open shelters. They then gathered book donations and held a public poetry festival to raise awareness and public ownership of the space.

In 2006 the federal government contributed funding for Magdeburg to construct a permanent building on the vacant site. The budget was lean and the project scrappy; architects used pieces from the facade of a recently demolished 1960s building to clad the new library. But by 2009 the city had a new library space as well as a manicured green lawn and public stage. The building provides shelter but is never closed—it uses overhangs and alcoves rather than doors to protect the collection donated by patrons. There is no librarian or staff: patrons borrow and return books freely on their own. The shared space is used for readings, gigs, and plays put on by the local elementary school. In 2010 the Magdeburg Open-Air Library jointly won the European Prize for Urban Public Space. It shared the prize with the Oslo Opera House, a project with a budget of over five hundred million euros.

In Newmarket, the city had already invested over $10 million in an attractive riverwalk park designed to draw residents together, and further public funds were limited. When a local financial firm offered to fund the construction of a book exchange building, the city matched that offer with donated employee labor. A local architecture firm contributed design work pro bono.

What they created is eloquently described by Alex Bozikovic, writing in the *Globe and Mail*:

> It sits in a quiet end of the park as a black box, harmoniously pro-portioned and precisely detailed, wrapped in a rhythmic screen of wooden slats. Its two hinged wings close up at night, leaving a glow-ing, translucent window to suggest what's inside; during the day it swings open like a dollhouse to reveal mahogany benches on each side, comfortable places to sit and browse through the titles on offer. (2015)

The Story Pod can be removed by forklift during Ontario's long, harsh winter. During spring, summer, and fall it's open seven days a week, twelve hours a day. The pod is used by local families as well as by the city's Parks and Recreation department programs, and it provides a signature element to the park, communicating Newmarket's commitment to com-munity, literacy, and design.

Key Principles: Why It Matters to Libraries

Conditions and Causes

The problems of Magdeburg and Newmarket were superficially very different—one a centuries-old industrial city with a struggling economy, the other a small suburb working to define itself as a distinct community on the periphery of a megacity. But both places needed to reinvigorate an ailing or underused public space and visibly assert their commitment to cultural and civic engagement. Both cities lacked the funds to invest in what they might have assumed they needed: a new library building, a collection to fill it, and salaries for its staff.

Many libraries face similar problems. We might be doing just fine, but we want to do better. We want to renew our spaces, services, and collections. Like the founders of PARK(ing) Day, we want to affect people's perceptions about big social issues like literacy, community, and the public good. These kinds of goals can feel unreachable if they seem to depend on large capital infusions—on raising the millions of dollars it takes to build a new library and fill it with purchased books and paid staff, or hiring public relations firms to launch an awareness campaign. Although it's important to note that not all libraries can be replaced by community book-lending and gathering spaces, there are important lessons here for the more traditionally staffed and funded libraries that sustain us.

The Nature of the Intervention

The Magdeburg Open-Air Library fully embraced the tactical values of *proof of concept* and *staged process*. It was first realized as a full-size scale model built of borrowed beer crates. From one perspective, creating a "fake" building out of temporary materials was frivolous, costly (in terms of time and effort), and meaningless. After all, it was just going to be taken apart. But seeing the scale model allowed the community to visualize the finished product and helped build community engagement and goodwill. It helped the group break a potentially overwhelming project into a series of achievable goals, which in turn helped build intangibles like *optimism* and *openness to new ideas*.

Rather than simply reproduce the structure and services of the existing Newmarket Public Library, the architects who designed the Story Pod spent time closely examining the city's needs and reframing the problem. This intellectual labor took longer than simply accepting a brief to "build a library," but it allowed the city to create a truly *local solution to a local problem*. It also helped the project stay within its limited budget and achieve a unique and beautiful result.

Both Magdeburg and Newmarket built *innovative partnerships*. In Magdeburg, city officials, architects, developers, and residents worked together to create and execute their plan. They staged their work carefully to guard against setbacks and disappointments in the community because public engagement was central to the project's success. And they successfully attracted partner funding from the federal government by first demonstrating their own commitment, resourcefulness, and creativity. In Newmarket, it was private funding partners who first brought the idea to city officials after seeing an inspirational project in Los Angeles. But the city expanded that partnership from within its own ranks. *ArchDaily* wrote, "Town of Newmarket employees, none of whom are full-time professional contractors, dedicated their work days in a cordoned off corner of a municipally owned machine shop to build the pod" (2015).

Both projects married the worlds of *practicality* and *experimentation*. As Shannon Mattern wrote of Little Free Libraries in *Places* magazine, "Often these are spaces of experimentation, where new models of library service and public engagement can be test-piloted, or where core values can be reassessed and reinvigorated" (2012). The same applies here. Neither Magdeburg nor Newmarket could afford a fully staffed, traditional library. But perhaps neither of them really needed it. Or perhaps these projects will prove to be one step in a longer road toward even more experimental, mobile, and flexible solutions.

LIBRARY MEETS CITY CASE STUDY 2:
THE L!BRARY INITIATIVE

NOT ALL TACTICAL LIBRARY PROJECTS ARE DONE ON A SHOESTRING. LOW BUDget and low threshold are important characteristics of a tactical intervention, but they're also relative concepts. The L!brary Initiative is an example of how large, complex, and relatively well-funded organizations can still use a tactical approach to overcome problems and accomplish goals.

New York City's public school system faces many challenges. In a city of over eight million, the system manages almost nine thousand schools across all five boroughs. According to the system's own statistics, every single borough has a majority of its students living in poverty. Brooklyn and the Bronx are in deepest trouble, with 87.9 percent of Bronx public school students and 77.5 percent of Brooklyn public school students living in poverty (New York City Department of Education, n.d.) The educational challenges of poverty are what brought the New York public school system to the attention of the Robin Hood Foundation, a nonprofit charitable granting organization dedicated to overcoming poverty in New York City.

The Robin Hood Foundation (though perhaps aptly named in the context of tactical interventions) is no guerrilla outfit. Founded in 1988 by a philanthropic hedge fund manager, it has an illustrious and well-heeled board of directors that has included Gwyneth Paltrow, Harvey Weinstein, Diane Sawyer, and the founders and CEOs of many major financial and charitable organizations. George Soros made a $50 million gift to the organization, and artists such as the Rolling Stones and Lady Gaga have performed at its benefit concerts. The foundation does what it calls "venture philanthropy," working strategically to maximize the return on its charitable investments by setting clear goals and targeting the recipients most likely to benefit from assistance.

In 1997 Lonni Tanner, director of special projects for the Robin Hood Foundation, began making the rounds in New York's design, financial, and education circles. The project she described seemed like a pipe dream: find a one-size-fits-all way to build literacy, community, and opportunity for poor children and their families across the five boroughs.

But Tanner wasn't dreaming. She had a very specific plan in mind: to reimagine and redesign the outdated, undersupplied libraries in New York City's low-performing public elementary and middle schools. In partnership with the Department of Education and major donors, the foundation planned to target the schools that showed the most need and potential to benefit from aid. It planned not only to equip their libraries with books and equipment but to staff them with highly qualified librarians and to design beautiful, unique spaces that would inspire students to engage and learn.

In keeping with its strategic approach, Robin Hood focused on libraries rather than classrooms, labs, or other school spaces because, as Tanner and others at Robin Hood frequently point out, "a library occupies only 5 to 10 percent of a school's total real estate, but serves 100 percent of its students and teachers, as well as parents and local neighbors" (Lau 2002). And in keeping with its business-oriented insistence on success, the foundation planned to work with expert partners every step of the way.

To navigate the school system bureaucracy, Tanner and her team worked directly with the office of New York City School Chancellor Howard Levy—a well-respected educational innovator and the very top of the public education ladder. To re-create the school library spaces, the team engaged internationally renowned Pentagram Design, responsible for updating the look of Saks Fifth Avenue and the design identity of the Savoy Hotel in London. Publishers Scholastic and HarperCollins each donated a million books to revive the libraries' collections.

Architecture, technology, construction, and financial firms provided in-kind donations, while professional artists worked with students and schools to design murals, friezes, signage, and other visual elements for each library. Last but not least, Tanner's team reached out to Syracuse University's Master's in Library and Information Science program to codesign a graduate program specifically for the librarians who would work in the L!brary Initiative schools. These librarians would complete their degrees while working in the schools and would be charged with providing service not only to the children in the school but to the teachers, staff, and students' families as well.

It was an ambitious and holistic plan, and it took time. A first cohort of ten libraries was completed in 2003, with twenty-one more following in 2005 and twenty-five more in 2007. As of 2016, a total of sixty-two school libraries in New York City had been remade, along with complementary projects such as a library garden and a summer reading camp.

The L!brary Initiative has been successful by almost any measure. As early as 2002, *Library Journal* wrote, "there's already quantifiable evidence that the library is playing a key role in improving students' academic test scores. Last fall, fifth graders at the predominantly Hispanic and African-American school demonstrated a 12 percent hike in their citywide social studies achievement exams" (Lau 2002). Former L!brary Initiative director Anooradha Iyer Siddiqi lists accomplishments including the establishment of secure funding for librarian and paraprofessional positions; the development of architectural design standards for elementary schools in New York City; and improved attitudes, moral support, and awareness of the importance of school libraries from all partners. From a design standpoint, the libraries have been recognized with at least eight awards from the American Institute of Architects, including a special citation for Lonni Tanner (Kolleeny 2005).

Perhaps most telling of all, the L!brary Initiative helped inspire and inform a similar renovation of school libraries in another city. The Baltimore Elementary and Middle School Library Project (aka the Baltimore Library Project) renovated thirteen high-need elementary and middle school libraries over the course of five years through a partnership between a private foundation, the public city school board, architecture and design firms, community groups, and others.

Key Principles: How It Speaks to Tactical Urbanism

Conditions and Causes

The problems of America's public education system are complicated, complex, and wicked, the subject of countless books and studies. In New York and other major American cities, the economic and political challenges are particularly fierce. As financial inequity grows, so do the achievement and opportunity gaps between the children of the wealthy and the poor. Race, too, figures in. Research by the Civil Rights Project at the University of California, Los Angeles shows that "segregation for blacks among all public schools has been increasing for nearly two decades," and reflects increasing trends of racial segregation as parents seek out alternatives such as charter schools and voucher systems (Civil Rights Project, n.d.).

All this is overwhelming enough to contemplate—but the Robin Hood Foundation has an even larger mission. Its purpose, simply put, is to fight poverty in America's largest city. Fixing the public education system is just one piece of that larger project. Even if the foundation were somehow able to overhaul the entire New York school system, that would only strike off one of poverty's thousand heads. Housing, health care, jobs—the foundation battles on all these fronts. The scope of the problems it addresses is so vast that even through the businesslike lens of "venture philanthropy" it's hard to imagine what success might look like.

The Nature of the Intervention

Like the Green Guerrillas movement, the Robin Hood Foundation cut an overwhelmingly large challenge down to size by focusing on a *smaller, more manageable set of problems* that would contribute to a larger strategic goal. The foundation had already identified early childhood education as a high-impact arena for fighting poverty. Narrowing its focus even farther, to high-need, high-potential elementary and middle school libraries, just made sense given the foundation's insistence on maximizing its resources.

The foundation further broke the project down into several cohorts, completing the work on each one according to a *carefully planned set of stages*. That approach helped reduce what was an overwhelming mandate to a manageable project with concrete goals and visible indicators of success. The scheme also helped reduce the potential for expensive oversights and errors because problems could be discovered and fixed along the way, and everyone involved could learn as they went.

Despite the deep pockets, professional know-how, and vast network of the Robin Hood Foundation, the L!brary Initiative project could not have happened without solid and diverse *partnerships*. Rather than try to re-create expertise in all the areas that would affect the project, the foundation formed partnerships with outside experts. Those partners contributed everything from financial, in-kind, and pro-bono resources to the validation and buy-in that schools and libraries need if they are to resonate with local residents and succeed.

It may seem odd to call library redesigns costing $400,000 to $500,000 "shoestring," but given the vast costs of any capital project, it's fair to say that the L!brary Initiative was done with *minimal financial resources*. Like Janette Sadik-Khan making parklets out of paint and bollards, the Robin

Hood Foundation used what it had at its disposal to the greatest possible effect. Each of the libraries was only 1,500 to 2,000 square feet, and most projects focused on interior design and renovation rather than new construction. Although the foundation's resources are far greater than what most people—or even cities—could offer, it spent sparingly and wisely to get the biggest bang for its buck. That approach obviously allowed its money to go farther. It also shows what's possible—and replicable—with the right people and organizations involved. Not every city has a star-studded poverty-fighting foundation like Robin Hood, but it's clear that money was not the only (or even the key) factor in the success of the L!brary Initiative.

LIBRARY MEETS CITY CASE STUDY 3: LIBRARIES PARTNERING FOR ARTS AND CULTURE

OUR THIRD LIBRARY-MEETS-CITY CASE STUDY IS A BUNDLE OF SEVERAL PROJ-ects showing how libraries have creatively partnered with artists and arts organizations to bring value to their communities. Artists and tactical urbanists have a lot in common—subversiveness, passion, creativity, and tight budgets. Indeed, projects like PARK(ing) Day and the Astoria Scum River Bridge show that artists and tactical interventionists are often the same people. Librarians have found ways to partner with artists, art studios, and cultural organizations to bring tactical interventions to life in the library and the city.

Cleveland Public Library: "See Also"

The Cleveland Public Library's cleverly named See Also project isn't exactly low budget, but it is ingenious, delightful, and intentionally ephemeral. It's the happy outcome of a generous gift from an arts-loving donor and library trustee that has provided funds for everything from an arts lecture series to staff professional development. In 2010 the library's See Also program began to host ambitious temporary art installations during the summer months in partnership with local nonprofit public works studio LAND. As of this writing, the library has mounted seven exhibitions in the reading garden of its main downtown branch.

The annual installations are chosen for their artistic merit as well as their relevance and appeal to the Cleveland community. The 2010 exhibition, titled *Watership Down*, was a collection of fragmented, fractured pieces of houses evoking the trauma of losing one's home as well as the hope of finding a new one. The 2013 installation, titled *The Reading Nest*, used discarded and salvaged planks from the city's industrial neighborhoods to weave an enormous gold-painted griffin's nest. (The griffin is a widely used design motif of the library's main branch building.) Thirty feet wide by eleven feet high, the nest had two openings that invited library patrons to wander inside, sit, and read, talk, or enjoy the space. The 2016 show, titled *#flockCLE*, took over the whole facade of the building as well as much of the surrounding public square and mall with brightly colored and whimsical snails, wolves, meerkats, and more. Each exhibition becomes a lively, delightful part of the public space for just a few months before it's de-installed.

Forest Park Public Library: Summer of Exploration Participatory Art Project

A lower-budget version of a tactical arts intervention appeared as part of the Forest Park (Illinois) Public Library's 2016 Summer of Exploration program. In partnership with artist Elaine Luther, librarian Alicia Hammond crafted a set of large wooden letters spelling "EXPLORE" and mounted them temporarily on the library's front lawn. The letters were painted red, yellow, and blue in keeping with the library's summer program branding and were inspired by the work of Matthew Hoffman, a Chicago artist who installs large-format words and phrases in different locations.

Luther and Hammond explained, in a piece they cowrote for the *Library as Incubator* website, "We didn't just want to install art in front of the library. We wanted to create an event that encouraged the community to have a hands-on opportunity to get creative" (2016). Shortly after the work was installed, Luther and Hammond set up a table of painting supplies and invited passersby and library patrons to make their mark on the letters. Although some people hesitated at first, the letters were soon brightly decorated by the community. Luther commented, "Normally that section of lawn at the library is just that—lawn, you just walk past it. We made it a place where people came together, made art, had conversations, crossed barriers. People slowed down and had a moment of unexpected beauty in their day" (Vogel 2015). The community-painted sign stayed up as long as the summer program lasted, then was retired.

Hennepin County Library: "Stop, Look, Art"

The Hennepin County Library in Minnesota has an enviable collection of public art, thanks to the county's long-standing One Percent for Art program requirement for building projects over $1 million. Following years of commissioning, selecting, acquiring, and installing public artworks, the library developed the Stop, Look, Art program to catalog the work and bring it to the public's attention.

Coordinating librarian Michele McGraw led the project, which involved the creation of a digital database of works and a documentary for local public television, exploring some of the pieces in greater detail. Students at the Minneapolis College of Art and Design were hired to photograph the works, with funds provided by Minnesota's Arts and Cultural Heritage Fund. Library staff provided in-kind support to catalog the work and create a digital database.

Hennepin County Library's art collection includes everything from massive mobile sculptures (a sixteen-foot hanging piece titled "Wind and Water Chime" in the main room of the Nokomis Library) to pastels, watercolors, and photography. The Stop, Look, Art project documents and reveals the collection to a larger audience through an ingenious partnership of agencies.

Prospect Heights Public Library: "Intersection | Prospect Heights" and "Brooklyn Transitions"

Since the early 2000s, the Brooklyn neighborhood of Prospect Heights has seen big changes in its population demographics and neighborhood landscape. What was once a majority black neighborhood has become increasingly white and wealthy, and in the last few years major developers have moved in and begun what one commentator calls a "phase four" of gentrification, with ultrarich, nonresident buyers scooping up multimillion-dollar investment real estate they never inhabit (Disser 2014).

In recognition of this trend and its negative impact on the neighborhood, the Brooklyn Public Library partnered in 2015 and 2016 with urban design studio Buscada and the Prospect Heights Neighborhood Development Council to mount a series of events and programs on the topic of gentrification. Titled "Intersection | Prospect Heights," the project drew on photographic and reporting work in the neighborhood by Gabrielle Bendiner-Viani, founder of Buscada, to create guidebooks that "show neighborhood places through the eyes of residents in the early 2000s" (Buscada 2015). Guidebooks were distributed throughout the neighborhood at local meeting spots like the library, shops, cafés, and restaurants—and were made available online for download. Residents were also invited to join in public discussions and neighborhood walking tours, view pop-up exhibitions, and record their own stories by making an appointment with the library.

Prospect Heights Neighborhood Development Chair Gib Veconi told the library that "valuing everyday experience and perceptions of place can help us create space for dialogue on the forces shaping our city. We hope the approachable form and personal narratives of this project will let participants laugh, cry and grapple with the experience of what is too often framed as the city's inevitable trajectory" (Brooklyn Public Library 2015).

For the Brooklyn Public Library, the Intersection | Prospect Heights project was part of a larger project encompassing the whole borough, titled "Brooklyn Transitions." In 2015 and 2016, the library hosted a series of events related to housing affordability and gentrification throughout Brooklyn. Booktalks, film screenings, panels and speakers, and oral history recordings all took place in and around the library, creating another venue for residents to address the changes in their neighborhoods.

Key Principles: How It Speaks to Tactical Urbanism

Conditions and Causes

In times of ease (Forest Park's summer programs) and of trouble (the increasing inequity in Brooklyn), artistic and cultural expression offer people a way of speaking their truth, learning from each other, and building stronger communities. Art contributes liveliness, beauty, and depth to human experience. A strong arts program can help a library reach through its walls to engage users in new ways—through a practice they admire or share, through admiration for the work, through revelation and deeply felt emotion. Art can enliven spaces and create room for new dialogue. It can offer whimsy and delight or foster solemn contemplation and reflection.

But libraries don't often write job descriptions for full-time practicing artists. Being an artist doesn't demand an MFA, but it usually takes some degree of skill, commitment, and aptitude as well as resources such as time and disposable income. Curation, art documentation, and even art handling all demand specialized skills, training, and equipment. Just as it's not possible for every librarian to also be an early education specialist or fluent in five languages, it's not possible to expect librarians to run full-fledged arts engagement programs on top of their other jobs. And that means that libraries can miss out on a broad avenue for welcoming members of the community into the library.

The Nature of the Intervention

Each of the libraries in this case study recognized the strength and expertise of arts organizations and professional artists who can contribute to the library's mission. Through *temporary partnerships and short-term projects*, each library gained something that it could not have provided solely for itself—eye-catching visual appeal to invite new people into the library, a professional record of the library's arts investment, a credible connection to community members feeling frustrated and betrayed by government institutions.

A few of these partnerships and projects generated physical artifacts—works of art, guidebooks—that stuck around after the term of the project was over. Some didn't. In all cases, what mattered more than the physical work created were the *intangible relationships and benefits*. The Cleveland Public Library invests big money in its gorgeous temporary art exhibitions, only to dismantle them when the summer is over. The Brooklyn Public Library spent money, staff time, and energy on organizing conversations, screenings, tours, and exhibitions that left no lasting trace in the library itself. And the Forest Park Public Library built a colorful, sturdy, community-decorated sign that stood on the front lawn for only a couple of months. You might ask how these organizations could justify spending anything on ephemeral and immaterial products, especially when library budgets are perpetually under siege. From a tactical perspective, the enduring nature of the products matters far less than the intangible benefits of the projects—the relationships formed between people and the institution, the new perspective people took on the library when they engaged with the art or events, the conversations generated between community members, and the learning of everyone involved. Sometimes the invisible and intangible products are the most valuable and enduring— indeed, often they are the primary goal of the intervention.

Several of these projects leveraged partnerships with art and cultural entities to create *broader networks of participation and ownership* for the library's offerings. The Hennepin County Library used the skills of fine arts students to photograph its art collection, exposing it to a broader community of library users (including those who might never have set foot into the library's buildings). The Brooklyn Public Library joined Buscada, the Prospect Heights Neighborhood Development Council, and others to reach neighborhood residents in such places as cafés, restaurants, and shops. Those residents were encouraged to share their own stories and help the project grow. Successful tactical interventions seek not just to connect with the local community but also to foster a sense of shared ownership and involvement. That's how projects like PARK(ing) Day take off at a national level, by giving participants the ability to own their level of involvement and offering ways for them to build the project out in new directions.

Last, each of these projects took advantage of the *passion and enthusiasm* of library staff and their arts and culture partners. In Forest Park, Alicia Hammond was charged with community outreach and engagement—

but nobody told her she had to do that by designing and fabricating big wooden letters for the library's front lawn. In Brooklyn, library staff could have chosen a less touchy and political issue to engage the community and steered clear of sticky, tricky discussions about race, money, and gentrification. But in both cases, librarians chose to jump in where they felt called to do so—inspired by the provocative work of an artist or by the clear need of the community to tackle a tough issue. Tactical interventions find their wellspring in the energy and initiative of their participants.

LIBRARY MEETS CITY CASE STUDY 4: LIBRARY BUILDING AND RENOVATION PROJECTS

OUR FINAL CASE STUDY SHOWS THREE WAYS THAT LIBRARIANS HAVE USED tactical approaches in some of the largest and most costly and time-consuming projects that we regularly face: renovations and new buildings.

Even as technology changes the role of the public library, decreasing its importance as the sole gatekeeper and repository for information, the library itself remains a vital civic institution. In recognition of this fact, many cities have invested in high-design "destination libraries," spending millions of dollars on new buildings and branches in the hopes of elevating their profile with both residents and tourists as well as branding themselves as places that value learning and education. Some cities have seen positive payback from this—Seattle's Rem Koolhaas–designed Central Library "opened to the public on May 23, 2004 and in its first year of operation attracted more than 8,000 visitors a day—double the average attendance in the old building" (Seattle Public Library, n.d.). Other cities have seen expensive, high-profile building projects flop. The New York Public Library hired Norman Foster to renovate its Central Library but canceled the project before the first book was taken off the shelf, due to criticism of the plan from within the library, the city, and the community (Rosenfield 2014). Clearly, a big budget doesn't guarantee a successful building project or its desired result: a vibrant, visit-worthy library.

For most libraries, that's beside the point—there's no big budget to start with. Most libraries operate on slender means and struggle to accumulate the capital for a big project like a new building or a renovation (see chapter 4's case study on Boston's Chinatown Storefront Library for an example of a library's decades-long difficulties finding money for a new library branch). Pulling together the budget and approvals for a library building project, whether it's renovating the reading room or constructing a new branch from scratch, is a demanding task for any librarian.

Building projects are big, long-term, and complicated. By law, they require multiple levels of expertise and official review. You can't expect to raise a new library building with an army of unskilled, enthusiastic community recruits—or if you do, you can't expect it to get permits or pass inspection. Surely library buildings are the last place you should expect to take a tactical approach.

Yes and no. It's true that building projects are a big deal and that they call for long-term strategic planning. But there are also ways in which a tactical approach can help. The following examples show how libraries have successfully combined tactics like iteration and experimentation, temporary solutions, and delightful design to tie big-picture strategy to local realities and produce elegant, functional libraries.

Tactical Renovation: D.C. Public Library Interim Branches

The city of Washington, D.C. is familiar with tight library budgets, especially for capital projects. In a system with twenty-six locations, there's never enough money to go around. When chief librarian Ginnie Cooper took over leadership in 2006, the district had spent years relying on cramped, out-of-date portable structures to serve the public when its permanent building projects couldn't be finished on time (Cooper 2010). A major overhaul was needed.

Many of the system's branch libraries were already under renovation, meaning they weren't available for public use. Some communities had been without functioning branch libraries for years. Cooper immediately made it a priority to restore service to these areas while their libraries were being rebuilt. Given the District's dispiriting history with portables, it was a bold move to do this by introducing more temporary libraries. But not all temporary libraries are alike.

The four interim libraries that Cooper and her team opened in 2007 were a mix of typologies—yes, some were in trailers, but others were in existing storefront buildings that the library system rented. Each of the interim libraries followed a consistent layout, with low shelving to maximize daylight and allow easy supervision of the space. A single service desk at the entrance welcomed patrons and helped establish staff presence and authority. Each temporary library was about four thousand square feet, with few interior walls and plenty of flexible spaces for patrons and cross-trained staff. And each of the temporary libraries was branded in the same way, with the same colors and signage and with a large, colorful banner stationed outside the front door to draw the attention of local residents.

Library staff made a concerted effort to situate the interim libraries where they would be discovered and used; in many cases, this meant as close as possible to the existing branches under renovation. Staff also went out into the community to spread the word about the new locations. Cooper wrote,

> Librarians visited schools and day-care centers, manned tables at community events, and invited community organizations into the new library. As construction began, family-friendly employment information fairs were held near the interims so that residents could learn about the library and potential employment. Word of mouth did its work, too. (2010, 6)

The interim library model proved to be a successful, low-cost way to provide continuous library service during the renovation of permanent library buildings. As planned and managed by Cooper and library staff, it reestablished trust with communities that had lost their connection to the library system and rebuilt habits of library use in neighborhoods that had felt abandoned by the system. The D.C. interim libraries also offer a replicable proof of concept for other libraries to borrow. As of 2010, the D.C. library system had opened four more interim libraries to bridge services for neighborhoods during renovation projects, and "the library board has made a commitment always to provide interim facilities while new libraries are under construction" (Cooper 2010, 6).

Tactical Renovation: Denton (Texas) Public Library North Branch, McAllen (Texas) Public Library, and Lebanon-Laclede County Library (Missouri)

Big-box retail stores have become a fixture of most American cities and towns, offering vast acreages of low-cost household goods, electronics, and even books in a single location. However you feel about our transition from human-scale Main Streets to car-focused strip developments, one thing is clear: when big-box retailers move or go out of business, they leave behind problematic urban design and architecture. Stores like Wal-Mart and Best Buy can easily occupy one hundred thousand square feet in a single building mostly undivided by internal walls, with lofty ceilings, minimal windows, and few amenities. Although they may work well as cheap retail warehouses, abandoned big-box stores are a visual blight, a burden on surrounding businesses and communities, and a challenge to repurpose in almost any way.

Several public library systems have tackled this challenge, turning big-box building shells into welcoming and vibrant public library buildings. In Denton, Texas, the North Branch location of the Denton Public Library system occupies a former Food Lion grocery store. At almost thirty-three thousand square feet of uninspired, low-slung retail architecture, the building was a tough location to imagine turning into a vibrant community center. But library director Eva Poole was explicit in her brief to Minnesota-based architecture firm Meyer, Scherer and Rockcastle (MSR): "We wanted a warm, inviting place so people wouldn't just check out a book and leave" (MSR, n.d.).

MSR responded by turning the former grocery giant into a modernist jewel. The redesign surrounded the entire building in a glass curtain wall—essentially an ornamental, nonstructural glass "skin" fabricated in a grid of both translucent and transparent panels. Low-cost, low-maintenance landscaping (mainly rocks and grasses) contribute to the sleek, modern look of the facade. Inside, more glass panels serve as acoustic barriers between sections of the space, allowing daylight to penetrate as far as possible while creating zones for different types of users. The new building incorporates both a secondhand bookstore and a drive-through for patrons to drop off items. It opened in 2003 and was awarded an AIA Minnesota Honor Award in 2006. The renovation cost approximately $100 per square foot, a tremendous bargain compared to the cost of new construction.

Eight hours south and several years later, the McAllen Public Library in McAllen, Texas, took a page from Denton's book. In 2006 the city purchased an empty WalMart building for $39 per square foot, tackling an even bigger challenge than the Food Lion had presented. The building was 123,000 square feet—an unthinkable size for a single-story library building. But McAllen had seen the success of Denton's North Branch Library and went back to MSR for the renovation. MSR added windows and skylights to brighten the interior space, provided plenty of electrical outlets, and hung huge three-dimensional, bilingual section signs to orient people and help bring the high ceilings down to human scale. Together with native landscaping, the changes turned what had been a desolate retail ruin into a vibrant community gathering place. In 2012 *Slate* wrote, "Interim director Kate Horan says that the numbers of new registrations and book loans at the library are 'through the roof'" (Lametti and Waldman 2012). The McAllen Public Library opened in its new location in 2011 and was a 2012 winner of the Library Interior Design Award from the International Interior Design Association and the American Library Association.

Meanwhile, in Lebanon, Missouri, an entire community was gathering to turn an empty Kmart into a library, museum, and café where everyone could go. The project was decades in the making. After the community outgrew its former library space and a donor left seed money for a new one, the town went looking for a new location. The search for a new library began in the mid-1980s, but it still wasn't resolved by 1999 when the local Kmart closed, leaving its building vacant. At forty-one thousand square feet, the building was a challenge for all the usual reasons, but it was cheaper than the $6 million that planners had estimated a new building would cost. In 2002 city planners started seriously investigating the Kmart location, and plans were laid to renovate it into what would become the Peggy Palmer Summers Memorial Library, sharing space with the Lebanon Route 66 Museum and Maria's Route 66 Café.

Renovating the Kmart building was cheaper than building something new, but the city of Lebanon still didn't have all the money it needed for the project. So the community raised the funds itself—a total of $2 million, mostly in tiny increments. Patrons could purchase a gold leaf on a donor tree destined for the library's lobby for as little as $25. Those who couldn't afford that much could give coins to the student penny drive, which raised a total of $4,000. Asked to estimate how many donated, project manager Dan True replied, "It honestly probably would be easier to count the people in this town who didn't help" (Christensen 2008, 146). Not only did locals contribute hundreds of gold leaves to the donation tree, they made in-kind donations of everything from electrical and construction work to interior design and the artistic labor of crafting the donation tree itself.

The building was carefully renovated to ensure that it wouldn't look like the big-box store it had once been. The exterior was reclad and updated in bright primary colors, establishing a scheme that runs throughout the building. Architect Charlie Johnson came up with a concentric-circles design to soften the rectilinear shape of the space as well as to express the idea of concentric ripples spreading outward in water, or the outward movement of a shared idea. The building's renovated entry includes an expansive, semicircular facade in keeping with this theme, which is also visible in rounded soffits and moldings inside.

The Lebanon-Laclede County Library opened to the public in 2004, offering a vibrant new place for the community and its visitors to gather. According to Maria Stone, owner of Maria's Route 66 Café, it is "the best thing that has happened to this town in a long, long time" (Christensen 2008, 146).

Tactical Renovation and Building: The Idea Stores

In 2001 Tower Hamlets, London, was a neighborhood with problems. Although it was a near neighbor to wealth and opportunity in Canary Wharf and the city's financial center, Tower Hamlets itself was a forgotten and excluded area. A high proportion of its residents were Bangladeshi immigrants, many with low levels of educational attainment and few connections to opportunity. The unemployment level was almost 70 percent higher than in surrounding areas. And though the city's public library system had branches offering full services for adult literacy and families, uptake was poor. People who could benefit from library services simply weren't taking advantage of them.

To address the problem, the library council commissioned a massive user study (aka a "public library consultation exercise"; Wills 2003, 108). From mailed surveys and in-person interviews, it became clear that although residents of Tower Hamlets valued the idea of the library, it didn't meet their needs. They needed longer service hours to accommodate their busy working lives, and they wanted more digital offerings. They also clarified a key issue for the library: its buildings just weren't working.

Many of the local library buildings were former schools, remnants of an earlier architectural era that looked genteel and dignified, even stately, to many Western eyes but that read very differently to Bangladeshi immigrants. Heather Wills wrote, "For people who were failed by the school system, who did not achieve any qualifications, or even a basic level of literacy, returning to sit in a classroom, going through the same gates into that same, forbidding school building, would always be a turn-off" (2003, 109). Most of the branches were located away from central shopping districts, making them hard to visit. Further, many of the buildings had small windows raised above street level, obscuring what was happening inside. Wills comments, "Anyone nervous about entering into a new environment wants to see what's inside before stepping over the threshold" (109).

With this feedback in mind, the library council began considering options for renewing its buildings. Moving into central shopping districts brought the realization that the library would have to compete in appearance, appeal, and customer experience with high-end retailers such as Gap and Nike. To clear this high bar, the council engaged a marketing firm to create a new, competitive library brand and test customer responses to proposed environments. "We thought they'd go for the 'middle of the road' department store style of presentation—a nicer environment than the 'Council leisure centre' style but not as daunting as the top-of-the-range store. Serve us right for being patronising—people wanted the best," Wills wrote (2003, 111–112).

The first Idea Store, an entirely rebranded and reconceived branch library, was created in a renovated council office in Bow, northeast of Tower Hamlet. The location was small (about 3,700 square feet) and convenient to local shops and supermarkets. The council installed large windows and automatic doors, cleanly designed signage, and retail-quality lighting. Inside, uniformed, cross-trained staff offered friendly service to patrons throughout the building, not just from behind a desk.

The outcomes of this first "prototype" Idea Store were encouraging. Patron visits more than quadrupled, and print circulation increased by 40 percent. Computer use and class enrollment both skyrocketed. Bolstered by these findings, the team revised its brief with lessons learned and moved to build more Idea Stores. Now that the concept had been proved, it made sense to invest more money in renowned architect David Adjaye's designs for Idea Stores in Whitechapel and Chrisp Street. The newest Idea Store buildings feature gorgeous, multicolored glass envelopes that brand the space and clearly show the interior to the street, sheltering atriums and allowing plenty of daylight. As of this writing, there are five Idea Store locations, offering books, Internet, and courses in everything from vegetarian cooking to Photoshop for beginners.

Key Principles: Why It Matters to Libraries

Conditions and Causes

A new building or major renovation is a big opportunity, and it usually comes with a lot of change. Even if things are running perfectly smoothly and you're only building to grow, you'll have plenty on your plate as you decide how to adapt to your new space. More often, there are complex problems leading you to a new or renovated space.

In the case of London's Idea Stores, user studies revealed that the existing buildings were secretly (to library staff, at least) dysfunctional. Everything from their locations to their architectural style was discouraging patrons from visiting the library, for reasons that were invisible to library staff until they took steps to see things through their patrons' eyes. The symptoms were clear: low uptake rates even in a community that could benefit greatly from what the library had to offer. Many librarians might dismiss low engagement as a systemic, almost unfixable problem—a side effect of changing social attitudes and increasing competition from television, the Internet, and e-commerce. It took empathy, energy, and a lot of hard work for the library council to understand the role that the "perfectly good" library buildings played in keeping potential users out of the library and then to fix it.

In the case of the Denton, McAllen, and Lebanon-Laclede libraries, the communities clearly wanted and needed new library buildings but lacked the immense resources needed to start construction from scratch. At the same time, their towns had become unwilling hosts to the eyesores and economic drains of vacant big-box stores. Lacking capital funds and burdened by urban design headaches, these library systems could have thrown up their hands—after all, city zoning decisions were beyond their control, and not even the most talented team can conjure several million dollars from thin air. The approach these libraries took instead transformed two big, stubborn problems into one elegant, inspiring solution.

In Washington, D.C., long-standing budget and planning problems had resulted in organizational gridlock. Although there was widespread agreement that the library system needed new buildings, it seemed impossible to get there smoothly—or, in some cases, at all. The long-term loss of services in some neighborhoods compounded the problem, creating a breach of trust with the community. Even with solid leadership and a capital budget in place, the library had a long road to travel in order to restore services, rebuild community relations, and build new branch libraries that would reengage users. Thoughtfully designed interim libraries proved a winning strategy for a thorny set of problems.

The Nature of the Intervention

Although each of these case studies is different, all of them share a common theme of providing a thoughtful, carefully tailored *local solution to a local problem*. In London, the Tower Hamlet library council undertook the largest-ever study of public library users in the UK in order to learn that one of their biggest, most valuable assets had to be scrapped. (To their immense credit, council members took that feedback to heart and rebuilt their library branches from the ground up.) In Washington, D.C. the interim branch libraries were carefully situated where they'd be most visible and accessible to the community. And in Lebanon, Missouri, the whole town pulled together to identify and create not only a library but also a museum, café, and community gathering place that suited locals' interests and tastes and reflected local history.

No building project is ever truly cheap, but each of these projects shows a relatively low-cost approach to renewing library spaces. Purchasing and renovating disused big-box stores, if it's done right, is cheaper than building from scratch, as Traci Lesneski's research shows:

> The cost to buy and renovate a Wal-Mart store into a library is roughly $175/sf (not including furnishings and other costs, such as fees, testing, etc.). Although construction costs vary with scope (e.g. quality, size, and location), the median construction cost for a high quality new library in the United States is $274/sf not including land costs. (2011, 399)

The interim libraries in Washington, D.C. were created in leased storefronts or trailers, with standardized layouts that made them quick and low-cost to set up. And in London, the first Idea Store was a renovation of an existing office space—no high-design "starchitect" or building budget was attached until later.

The Lebanon-Laclede library is a stellar example of creating a *distributed ownership* model for a big project. Not only did library staff engage the whole community in funding the renovation, but they found a way for that funding and ownership to be visible and perpetually recognized through the giving tree in the library's entryway. The library, café, and museum were designed with the input and involvement of the whole community, creating a sense of shared ownership and ensuring that the services and spaces would be used.

In Washington, D.C. the interim branch libraries were designed to be not just low-cost and functional but also *easily replicable*. Their floor plans and layouts were consistent and easy to adjust to slightly different iterations depending on the location (a rented storefront or a trailer). The staffing, signage, branding, and workflows were all designed to work in multiple locations with minimal revision. Not only did replication save on costs, but it made for a quick, easy implementation each time the library needed a new interim branch—and meant that other library systems could easily follow the same blueprint.

The Idea Stores in London took a different tactical approach by creating a *prototype* location before going full-scale. Renovating an existing office space allowed the library council to try out ideas and phase out or adjust anything that wasn't working. Only when the prototype was a success did the council get out its wallet to hire an architect and build from scratch. Real-world prototyping let the library test what it learned from research and user studies with minimal investment before moving on to more high-cost phases of the project.

Following Up: An Interview with Ginnie Cooper

I SPOKE WITH Ginnie Cooper, the former chief librarian of the District of Columbia Public Library, about bookmobiles and bread trucks, the importance of a great library board, and getting a major public library system back on track.

What problems did you face with the D.C. public library renovations?
When I arrived July 1, 2006, I already knew a bit about the situation with the D.C. public library system. A couple of years before I was hired, the board had hired a firm to do a design-build scheme for most of the neighborhood libraries. That scheme included emptying and shuttering the existing libraries that were to be replaced. Four libraries had been shuttered and were just sitting there, closed to the public until I could get something done. The board suc-

ceeded in overturning that design-build contract and was thinking about how they would fund really good libraries. So it was less about "Oh, this would be a good idea," and more about "Oh my God, we've got to do this."

At that time, the D.C. library system was viewed as pretty awful by many members of the public. So the communities were not surprised but were disappointed to have their libraries shuttered.

We worked very hard with our partners in other D.C. government to change that perception of libraries. The firm that had the design-build contract gets some of the blame for all the crapola, but in reality they didn't have enough money to do more than cookie-cutter suburban-style libraries in suburban settings. I'm so glad those buildings didn't get built as they were designed.

How did you address the problems? What resources did you have, and what helped the most?

The first thing I did was find a book-mobile and put it in place so it would immediately offer something to those communities. We did that in four to six months. But a bookmobile is like a bread truck that turns up on your block once a week for a couple of hours—when it shows up, do you know to run out and buy bread? Not necessarily. So it was a start, but it wasn't enough.

I had a really great board and a great board chair. They were able to convince the mayor and city council that more money was needed. We got a book budget and then the interim libraries were our next step.

We researched the fastest way to do this. We had a minimum size for those interim libraries. Some were in store-fronts and some were built by a firm that does mobile classrooms. Each interim library was maybe the size of two or three classrooms. One advantage of mobile buildings was that they could go on the site where the old libraries had been and the new libraries would go. We were able to place a couple of them in locations where they could stay throughout construction, which was wonderful.

How did you know if the interim libraries were meeting people's needs?

We made quite a lot of changes besides the interim library buildings. For instance, there had been AV [audiovisual] materials at the central library but no DVDs or other media, or books in other languages, in the neighborhood branches. We started buying that kind of material to supply those libraries. We also bought a lot of easy-reading material. There were quite low levels of literacy in some of those neighborhoods at the time. We did multiple children's programs. We did outreach work to schools and day-care centers to draw them in and took programs out to them. We had no magic bullet but we did have a good panoply of user services.

To see how it was working, we tracked gate count and circulation. And we also knew that those neighborhood libraries are often places where people might go to spend the day or use the Internet but never check out a book to take home. So circulation counts alone won't show the full use. We learned a variety of other ways to measure use, which worked pretty well.

We also determined that those libraries would be safe and secure. When I started my position, there were uniformed guards at the central library but not at the neighborhood libraries, and some of them needed it. It meant something to have a friendly person in uniform greet you and your child, and to know that person was there to greet your child if he visited by himself.

I think we redesigned eighteen libraries in the seven or eight years I was there. Because of the trouble before I arrived, the library board adopted the following policy: no neighborhood libraries would ever be closed again for renovations without having interim libraries in place.

This was an innovative and unusual project. How did you create buy-in?
We thought of everything as a blank slate, and we made it a priority that we would provide what library users wanted as quickly and easily as possible. That was a real change for the library system. Previously the system had few ways to identify work that needed to be done, set expectations of staff performance, create accountability, or offer training or appreciation. People who did good work did it because they decided for themselves it needed to be done. So you had some people who had truly given up because there was no reward of any kind. There was actually often a countermeasure, with old staff criticizing newer, hard-working staff who made them look bad.

We hired a fair number of new people, and we found the early adopters. If you reward them and let them have success, then that group gets bigger and bigger as other people see what's possible. Lots of people who cared about the library were empowered to make it right in ways that took us everywhere. Library staff met with community groups—it

was expected of branch managers. Some folks were spectacular at that. That helped to recruit library users and supporters. That's what really makes it happen.

I didn't know for years if it had worked or would work. D.C., within our profession, had been understood to have the worst library system in the country. And all of us in public libraries hated the fact that our federal elected officials saw that library system as the exemplar for the country. I went in thinking *I don't think I can do what is needed to improve this library.* In the early months, I thought about leaving several times a week. But I had a very good board, some fabulous staff, strong support from many local elected officials, and enough money to do most of what we wanted.

We also had Friends of the Library groups that were very supportive and worked with us to do good things. The first time we had a Friends group testify in support of us was a major thing— usually the Friends group would just complain that the D.C. library wasn't being supported well enough compared to other places.

We offered city council members and mayoral folks plenty of opportunities for praise and recognition for the work they did for the library—laying the first brick, attending groundbreaking ceremonies, shelving the first book, and so on.

What advice do you have for library leaders who want to use a temporary or interim library space as part of their library?
Think carefully about the purpose of it. In some places we could replace a library and in others we could offer a space for

children's programs, readings, and other programs in churches, community centers, or other locations. Know how long the interim library will be in use. Have a clear plan for what will replace it as soon as possible.

One of the things that has helped me is that I was flexible about my exact definition of success. If I can't get to this goal, can I get to this goal?

We did very well. We had way more successes than I thought we would in building the new buildings. We were lucky in lots of ways. That flexibility of how you define success—not being wedded to one method or one goal—is key.

And tactical urbanism was always on our mind. We were always asking ourselves, what difference does the library make to our neighborhood and city—what role are we playing in the city's goals around education, economic development, and technological improvement? What is our role and how can we be a partner to local government in a way that serves everybody?

Following Up: An Interview with Eva Poole about the Denton (Texas) Public Library

I TALKED WITH Eva Poole, former director of the Denton Public Library system, about grocery stores, drive-through book pickup, and the perfect shade of red for library walls.

What made you choose a big-box renovation for Denton? What factors made it appealing and possible?

Years ago the Food Lion grocery store chain went through a controversy that resulted in many of its Texas stores closing. Because of that, a Food Lion store in our northern service area in Denton became available. It was an ideal location for a branch of the Denton library because at the time we only had one branch located on the opposite end of town. Also, grocery stores tend to be where they're most needed and where people can reach them. This store was adjacent to a middle school, across the street from a park, and an ideal location for a neighborhood library. I first met with my board and expressed the need for a second library branch in the northern part of the city. In a collaborative process, we worked with the city council and members of city management, and we all agreed that the Food Lion location would be perfect for a library. As a result of inclusion and listening with members of the community, the bond issue for library improvements was issued by the city, and funding was voted on by the citizens at large and overwhelmingly approved for funding. I believe the approval rate was more than 77 percent of the number of votes cast.

What were the conditions you were dealing with?

We started working with an architect from MS&R [Meyer, Scherer and Rockcastle]. The problem with grocery stores is that they all look alike. It's great for recognizability when it's a grocery store, but we had to work together to make sure that that utilitarian design would be nonrecognizable. Even the parking lot—how could we redesign that sea of concrete and add green space on the site, while preserving adequate parking for the library?

I remember walking through the grocery store building, every inch of it, imagining how we could utilize this space to make it a library. The building was huge with lots of available square footage. We decided we could move our cataloging and processing staff from our Central library to the North Branch. It became our system-wide location because we had so much available space for both staff and public services.

What resources did you have? If you didn't have enough, how did you make it work anyway?

I think the bond measure gave us about $6 million, which was adequate funding for most of what we wanted to do. Other external funding came from the Friends of the Library and donations from citizens. We did have to change contractors for a portion of the project and reduce some of the original design elements in the building, but we made the funding work and stayed within the allotted budget.

What did you want to accomplish?

We wanted to make the library accessible to as many people as possible whether we were open or closed. We wanted no barriers of access so that people could easily use library resources. I personally wanted a place that made people feel like they could stay in the library all day if they wanted to do so, because it was such a beautiful building. My public library when I was growing up was my refuge, and I wanted to extend that feeling of a safe place to the whole

city in my community. And I think we achieved that goal in our new branch location.

In the public areas, we created window seats, especially in the children's area, so children could sit comfortably and read. Where the original loading dock had been, we created an adult area for quiet seating because it was far away on the opposite side of the building from youth services and also had a view of the park across the street. We were very aware of using the window spaces for people to access and enjoy.

We also thought about nurses, doctors, and people who worked nontraditional hours around the clock and who would want the library to be accessible to them as well. We installed 24/7 lockers in the building foyer, so customers could call ahead and get a locker combination to pick up their materials at a convenient hour for them. We also partnered with law enforcement and other city offices. We had a police officer housed in the building 24/7 so people would feel safe coming in to pick up their items when the library was closed. And there was a drive-through for busy mothers and other people to drop off materials without having to physically come into the building. Customers could call ahead, too, and arrange to pick up materials from the drive-through window. People utilized this service all of the time.

How did people respond to the renovation?

We had ten thousand people attend our grand opening day. It was a huge community-wide event. We had a lot of public art on display. We had the mayor and the city manager, city councillors, architects, library board and Friends organization members in attendance as well. A band played music, we had storytimes, face painting, tours of the building, and all kinds of programming throughout the day. We had this beautiful library building where a former Food Lion used to be located. We had created this impactful place that generated positive change in our community.

At that time I don't think many libraries used as much color on the walls to define the various areas of the library as we did. I heard one visitor at the opening day celebration say, *That red—I would never have done that!* So perhaps the beautiful, bright colors did contribute to the high circulation and usage of our new branch library!

This was an innovative and unusual project. How did you create buy-in?
There were many contributing factors. An efficient use of a building that was vacant and available for sale at a reasonable price. Also, the library only had one branch location at the time in the southern sector of town. No library services were available in the northern area of the city. We didn't have an integrated automated library system, and we consistently had people waiting in long lines to borrow items. We didn't have a large collection, either. With these factors in place, it was a pretty easy conversation to have with the community at large once we had an available building with the structural capacity to accommodate shelving and all of the equipment needed

for a library that we didn't have to build from the ground up. And most importantly, we had an existing building that would not remain a vacant, boarded-up eyesore in the community but would become a destination in the city for people to see and enjoy.

Working with the Master Gardeners we also created a garden out of the retention pond area. This garden contained native plants and stone benches for seating areas for the community to use as a "teaching" garden. The Master Gardeners funded the entire project.

What advice do you have for library leaders who want to undertake an innovative building or renovation project at their institution?
You have to involve your community. We had many focus groups, and we talked directly to people in the community. We held charrettes and brought people in to review the design of the new library. For a building project to be successful, you need the buy-in and support from your community. As the director, you can't drive the entire process without help from your staff. It's so much easier when community members go to their city councillor or city manager and make your case for you. Listen to your community. It wasn't just what we as library staff wanted in the new building, although we too had input. But the community really drove the design process, and that's why it was successful and why we had such an outpouring of excitement when the new building opened.

6

COMING BACK TO EARTH

FTER EXPLORING SO MANY EXAMPLES OF TACTICAL LIBRARY
interventions, you might feel that tactics can do any-
thing. I hope you have a sense of how flexible and adaptable a tactical mind-set is and a glimmering of how it
can transfer across different types of work. If the same
principles—start small, value intangibles, pursue partnerships, pursue your passion—can undergird projects as diverse as
LibraryBox, MarcEdit, and a redesign of more than sixty urban elementary school libraries, then surely they can help your own library, too.

I hope you're feeling inspired and charged up about tactics—I think it's
worth getting excited, especially because tactics tend to be so overshad-
owed by strategy in our professional culture. But just as we took a minute
in the beginning of this book to review some of the potential pitfalls of
a tactical approach, it's worth taking another minute now to temper our
excitement with reality. In this section we'll hit the brakes and consider
some of the limits of tactical interventions in library settings.

Sometimes Tactics Just Don't Work (the Way You'd Like)

You might come up with what you think is a great tactical solution to a problem—something you're willing to throw your heart and soul into—and it might flop. Maybe you invite the public to participate in a pop-up art installation, and nobody shows up. Maybe you write code to get your patrons around a known problem with your link resolver . . . and nobody pays attention. If your goal was to start small and grow big, it can be pretty demoralizing when a project fizzles.

Whether it's a problem with timing, execution, or uptake, some interventions will fail to pay off. You can minimize the chances of disappointment by following a few best practices (see chapter 8, "Twelve Steps to Becoming a Tactical Library Interventionist"), but you can never completely foolproof your project. Tactical interventions are, by nature, a bit of a risk. When you try something new and different, share ownership with others, and indulge whimsy and humor, you put yourself on the line. Take heart: big strategic projects fail too, and they cost a lot more to fix.

You might have to go back to the drawing board and try again, ideally after talking to plenty of people about what went wrong (or what didn't go right enough). Maybe next time you offer your pop-up at a different time of year, or in a different location, or invite a journalist who can write up your show in the local paper. Maybe you publish a piece about your code in a state, chapter, or regional professional association journal—or you share it on a discussion list for programmer analyst librarians. Or maybe you reshape your goals for your intervention and recall the words attributed to Thomas Edison: "'I have not failed 10,000 times. I have not failed once. I have succeeded in proving that those 10,000 ways will not work'" (Furr 2011).

Sometimes Tactics Work . . . And People Don't Like Them

Maybe you get people to turn out to a pop-up art exhibition, and the next day you're deluged with complaints because people think you should have spent money on children's programming instead. Maybe you write code to make your link resolver work better, and patrons reject it because they were used to the old system's quirks. Or maybe you stumble into a bigger set of problems—maybe people get angry or offended by something essential about what you're doing. Consider PARK(ing) Day—from one point of view it's a whimsical, provocative invitation to reconsider the role of automobiles in urban culture. From another it's an enormous pain in the neck, a goofy out-of-touch elitist art project, and a waste of time. (You can bet people have said all those things.) When you try out a tactical intervention, you need to prepare yourself for the possibility that you might get some hard feedback. Someone might object not just to your priorities but to the content of your art exhibition. Or they might criticize your code as kludgy and inelegant. What you say and do might come across to someone else in a completely different way from how you intended it, and both you and your library will need to deal with that.

Tactical Intervention Can Take a Lot Out of You

It's one thing to say that tactical interventions can be passion projects, driven by the enthusiasm and volunteerism of the participants. That's true—and it's also true that working on something you care about can feed your fire. But tactical projects often happen in the margins of the official—on meager budgets, in overload or out-of-class work assignments, or completely on your own time. In these situations, it's important to recognize that tactical interventions are work. Even if they're delightful and rewarding, they're still work. Whether a project is temporary or long-term, it takes resources to pull it together. And because tactical interventions happen in the margins, they often demand work that is unsupported by existing structures, budgets, relationships, and staffing. Tasks such as organizing volunteers and communicating with external partners tend to be particularly time-consuming. There may be no official way to recognize the merit and value of the work, if it happens outside position descriptions and evaluation rubrics. And if you're balancing a tactical intervention on top of a full-time job and maybe some unplanned additional duties, you might be headed for burnout.

Tactical Intervention Can Ask a Lot from You

Launching a successful tactical intervention can demand a wide range of skills. It is hoped that you've assembled a team of partners to help share the load, but there are some things you can't crowdsource. It takes courage to try something that's a little outside the organizational norm—to ask for money, time, staff, and leeway to do something different. It takes initiative and finesse to talk other people into joining your bandwagon. Dealing with setbacks demands humor and persistence. Answering skeptics takes a dash of oratorical skill. Accepting feedback gracefully requires an even keel. You can usually find partners to teach or contribute the hard skills you need, but launching a tactical intervention may mean stretching yourself out of your comfort zone in more than one direction.

Tactical Interventions Can Be Fragile

It's impossible to separate the cheapness, lightness, and quickness of tactical interventions from their fragility—they're two sides of the same coin. But that knowledge might not be very comforting when the budget you tenaciously scraped together disappears due to a new, competing priority, or when a partner drops out of the project, or when you're reassigned to a new strategic priority and you have to shelve the project or scrap it altogether. There's some freedom to operating on the edges of the official power structure, but the trade-off is that there are no guarantees. Big strategic directions sometimes get redirected too, but lightweight tactical projects are easier to abandon because they represent less investment. Don't be surprised if your project faces endangerment at some point in its life cycle—and be sure you have clear goals and a plan to transfer, sunset, or build on what you've created as long as you do have control over it.

Tactical Interventions Might Gloss Over Bigger Problems

This potential pitfall is a really tough one, but it's important to consider. As much as we might like tactical interventions for their scrappiness, their populism, and their style, we have to consider some fundamental questions of equity and privilege. Who gets to practice tactics, either in a city or a library? Who gets noticed and heard when they do try a tactical approach? When we talk about doing things on the margins of permissibility—whether it's tossing seed balls onto private property or setting up open-source Internet hubs in public parks—who's called a tactician, who's ignored altogether, and who's called a criminal?

Consider the Boston Street Project's Storefront Library. Decades of activism by the Chinese-American community haven't persuaded the city to open a new branch of the library. They haven't even made the news in any significant way. But when two wealthy, white, connected New Yorkers took up the cause, people paid attention. The Storefront Library is an excellent attention-getting departure from traditional library advocacy campaigns. But it's still important to ponder the underlying questions that it raises about privilege, voice, and attention.

How do we decide what's noteworthy, what's important, what's worth investing in and fixing? Whom do we consider a tactical interventionist? If, when we admire an ingenious intervention, we forget to critically consider the broader systems in which it exists, we are only distracting ourselves with a temporary solution to a much bigger, more enduring problem.

7

A LIBRARY LEADER'S GUIDE TO BUILDING A TACTICAL LIBRARY

F YOU'RE A LIBRARY LEADER—ANYONE FROM A STAFF SUPER-visor to a middle manager to a library director or dean—you may be wondering where you fit into all this tactical talk. After all, we've spent a lot of time talking about how tactics can operate outside traditional organizational structures, how tacticians can be gadflies to bureau-cracy, and how distributing ownership across the community of users can benefit tactical projects. Where does that leave the library administrator, even one who thinks tactics are a great tool to add to the institutional kit?

In a pretty great spot, actually. There's a lot that library leaders can do to help foster a tactical library culture—in fact, if administration is on board, projects can be that much lighter, quicker, and cheaper because they don't have to clear as many organizational hurdles or tiptoe through institutional minefields. Think of Janette Sadik-Khan, whose job was to administer the entire transportation system of New York City. That's a pretty hefty administrative task, and one that most of her predecessors had approached by fairly staid and conventional means—with long-term strategic plans, big budgets, and slow and considered projects. Sadik-Khan shook things up with her rapid-fire, lightweight (and, some would say, aggressive and abrupt) tactical approach. Sadik-Khan was no less a tactician or a disruptor because she held a bureaucratic appointment. Indeed, she used her position to advance tactical methods and to offer them new legitimacy and visibility in the context of a world-class urban system.

The other good news is that if you're a library leader whose staff want to try out some tactical interventions, that means you're already doing something right. Staff who want to try new things, who see and suggest ways to improve their workplace, are by definition engaged employees. Many library administrators struggle to build engagement and passion in their organizations—if your people already have it, count your blessings and do what you can to develop it. Of course, not every tactical notion is a good one, and there are both good ways (polite, collaborative) and bad ways (uncommunicative, unconsidered) to challenge conventions. But even if your would-be tacticians are a little rough around the edges, remember that they care about the organization and its success. If they didn't, they wouldn't be so darned pushy. As a library leader, you can help reward engagement, model respectful communication, and build working relationships to make the best of the ideas that your tacticians bring you.

As you may have noticed, much of what any good tactical intervention needs is intangible: the right approach, the right attitude, the right relationships, and, above all, the energy, time, and willingness to jump in. So let's explore how library leaders can help generate and protect these intangibles and create a tactics-friendly organization.

Handling Hierarchy, Bureaucracy, and Process

Traditional organizational processes get an implicit bad rap in discussions of tactical intervention. Most of the time that's because tactics are coming to the rescue in situations where bureaucracy has gone sour—where the needs of everyday people are being thwarted or ignored by a rule-bound or indifferent organization. It's easy for tacticians playing the role of gadfly to set themselves up against bureaucracy, hierarchy, and organizational process. Indeed, some tactical interventions are specifically intended to circumvent or expose the dysfunctions of bureaucracy.

That approach can create a challenge for even the open-minded, well-intentioned library administrator who's charged with maintaining organizational processes. If tacticians come on strong, it's easy for library leaders to respond with defensiveness and even anger or hurt feelings. Feelings of misunderstanding or bad faith can deteriorate into conflict, making a problematic situation even worse. What can library leaders do to strike a workable balance between process and tactics?

To begin with, it may be helpful to consider whether there's a legitimate problem with how your organization works. If staff propose a reasonable tactical intervention that's blocked by procedures or regulations, how valid are those procedures and regulations? How valuable are they when weighed against the potential benefit of the intervention? How important are the principles of consistency and precedent, compared to the potential outcomes of letting staff have ownership of a tactical project?

Administrators often have a system-wide view of the organization that staff in other positions lack, meaning that administrators sometimes see legitimate reasons to stick to established processes. They also sometimes see the benefits of process more clearly than do other staff. For both these reasons, it's important to communicate clearly with your tactically minded staff. If your objection to a pop-up art show and reception is partly that library funds can't be spent on food and drink, maybe your tacticians can help identify an alternative funding source or an in-kind donor, or maybe they'd be willing to plan their event as a potluck. Explaining your reasons clearly and showing a willingness to seek compromise may expose more middle ground than you thought you had.

Managing Tactical Personalities

Tactical interventionists tend to share several personality traits—a high level of energy, openness to new ideas and experimentation, and a tendency to be curious and proactive. These are the characteristics that lead tacticians to leap in and take responsibility where none is clearly assigned. And they're all great traits to have in your organization. In their essay "Proactivity in the Workplace," Chiahuei Wu and Sharon K. Parker wrote,

"Being proactive involves self-initiated efforts to bring about change in the work environment and/or oneself to achieve a different future" (2011, 84). They cite several studies showing the importance and value of proactive behavior at work, including a meta-analysis showing (not surprisingly) that "individuals with a proactive personality reported higher career success and job performance" (84).

A self-motivated, proactive approach to work is a big help in most libraries—so much so that we often list it as a desired trait in job descriptions. But there's also such a thing as taking too much initiative. Consider the example of Janette Sadik-Khan, New York City's commissioner of transportation, who cut miles of red tape and incited both delight and anger when she fast-tracked bike lanes and parklets in ways no one had ever seen before. Sadik-Khan jumped the line on city resources, okayed tasks without observing all the correct (or at least expected) procedures, and pushed projects through without always talking to all the stakeholders as much as they would have liked. A city councilwoman reported that colleagues found Sadik-Khan "dismissive and confrontational," but no one could deny that she got things done (Grynbaum 2011).

As a library leader, you may at times feel tested by the energy, curiosity, and engagement of staff who want to experiment with tactics. Even if we all agree that a proactive temperament is a plus, it can be frustrating to juggle institutional requirements with tactical personalities—even if those personalities come attached to good ideas. Sometimes it's the leader's job to pump the brakes, question the methods, or simply say no. It can take delicacy and a diplomatic touch to avoid creating the perception of obstructionism, which in turn risks demoralizing staff and losing all that valuable proactive energy.

Fostering (and Filtering) Passion

The passion project, otherwise known as the vocation, calling, or side hustle, has a large, probably underappreciated role to play in our work lives and even in our national economy. Classic examples of American passion projects are the garage start-ups of business juggernauts Apple and Nike.

Passion, which might also masquerade as frustration with the status quo, can drive people to build bridges over leaky pipes even though nobody's paying them to do it, or volunteer to step out of their office jobs and help build a site for reading and socializing in their city park. And there's a difference between being proactive and being passionate. Both are good, but passion will get you farther in the long run, because when people are driven by passion and a sense of purpose, they're going to act whether they're paid or not.

So what is passion in the context of the workplace—how do we define it, exactly? In their essay "Passion at Work: Towards a New Conceptualization," psychologists Robert Vallerand and Nathalie Houlfort describe workplace passion as "a strong inclination toward an activity that people like, that they find important, and in which they invest time and energy" (2003, 177). They distinguish obsessive passion from harmonious passion—the former is compulsive and harmful, the latter involves free choice and gratification. In other words, not all passion is good passion. We've all worked with a colleague who's so adamantly committed to excellence that she alienates her entire staff, or one whose vehement and vocal workplace frustration scares us away.

Furthermore, some researchers suggest that workplace passion is particularly likely to show up in an entrepreneurial context. Business professor Melissa Cardon and her research colleagues wrote,

> Passion is deeply embedded in the folklore and practice of entrepreneurship. Dating back to Schumpeter's early writings . . . , researchers and practitioners alike have invoked passion to explain entrepreneurial behaviors that defy reason-based explanations, such as unconventional risk taking, uncommon intensity of focus, and unwavering belief in a dream. (2009, 511)

In start-ups as well as in tactical interventions—both situations involving elevated levels of risk, uncertainty, and individual responsibility at work—passion is a big part of what sustains the practitioner.

It's important to recognize that passion is a common element in tactical projects and that it can be both a welcome fuel for the work and a dangerous potential source of friction. How do you foster the right kind of passion, the kind that generates energy without burning the place down? Cardon and her colleagues suggest drawing on the same drive that feeds the entrepreneurial or tactical spirit to help people self-regulate their passion. In other words, passionate people can use fire to fight fire through such tactics as setting clear goals and paying close attention to exactly what aspects of the project make them feel strongly.

Library leaders can help foster harmonious passion by establishing clear channels for communication across hierarchies and work groups as well as by considering creative methods such as administrative "pink zones" or design sprints to allow staff to test out their ideas.

Rewarding (Harmonious) Passion

All that said, the quickest way to extinguish someone's passion (including your own) is to exploit it. A cynical library leader might say, *Great, the staff are passionate about creating a new reading room and we have no budget—they can build it for free on the weekends.* It's true that proactive, passionate people will take on certain types of work—work that they feel strongly about—whether or not it carries a paycheck. But even harmonious passion will die out if the organizational leadership ignores, opposes, or capitalizes on the interventionist's passion without ever rewarding it.

Let's say that your library needs a new reading room and there's no budget for it, but plenty of passion exists among the staff to make it happen. How can an ethical library administration make use of that passion without exploiting it?

To begin with, of course, any library leader must make sure that fair labor practices, collective bargaining agreements, and other workplace policies are observed. Some libraries, for example, make a point of clarifying in writing that unionized employees are not expected to work (or even respond to e-mail) during nonworking hours. Others have clear guidelines about the kinds of duties that employees can take on without triggering additional pay. But assuming that these kinds of safeguards are in place, how does the cash-strapped administrator not just make room for people to work passionately but reward it appropriately?

In some situations, like the Astoria Scum River Bridge, the work is short-term and the scope is clearly defined. Here, one reward might be simply accomplishing the project itself and seeing it adopted by people who need it. In the case of the reading room, staff who feel strongly about the space might take some satisfaction from being allowed to improve it in minor ways that fit with their understanding of how the space is used.

Research tells us that people are more engaged and happier in their jobs when their work is seen as important and valuable—that is, it contributes to and is aligned with the success of an organization that shares and advances their own world views. Andrew Winston wrote in *The Big Pivot*, "There's an intrinsic or internal reward that people feel from having a sense of achievement, being valued, or finding meaning in the work itself. . . . Basically, people work harder and better when they care about what they're doing" (2014, 148). So there's a certain amount of payoff for most people in just being engaged as well as a payoff for the organization in having happier, more engaged, and more productive employees. Finding ways for people to do work they enjoy is a win-win for everyone.

Agency, engagement, and a sense of shared values are intrinsic motivators—they spring from within individuals themselves. Obviously, people also care about extrinsic motivators such as money and awards. Library leaders can recognize engaged performance at work, whether it's by explicitly appreciating employees' work or by connecting compensation to passionate engagement. Most libraries have budget, salary, and union labor restrictions that make it hard to offer the kinds of bonuses that reward employees in the corporate sector—but there's still a wide range of ways in which creative administrators can reward outstanding work.

Cinthya Ippoliti, writing in *Library Leadership and Management*, makes a basic but often-missed suggestion for administrators looking for ways to recognize staff:

> Begin by asking how people want to be recognized—for some, a simple thank you is enough, while for others, a big show of appreciation means much more than a private word. Knowing what each person prefers will help pave the way for you to give appreciation in a mean-

ingful and heartfelt manner as opposed to assuming you know the answer. (2016, 15)

Sending handwritten thank-you notes, praising staff in front of their peers, taking employees out for one-on-one time over coffee or lunch, upgrading work spaces or equipment, offering professional development opportunities, or even just making sure to pass along words of praise and enthusiasm are all ways to show people that their harmonious passion is appreciated at work.

Communicating Ideas

Leaders are uniquely positioned to help ideas get born, fostered, and shared in organizations. After all, leaders are key to creating corporate culture. They have a disproportionate impact on whether the organization feels easy or stuffy, rigid or fluid. Do people feel free to speak their minds, or is there a fear (maybe a well-founded one) of recrimination and backlash? Are there ways for staff to share information anonymously or confidentially—apart from the rumor mill that exists in all organizations? Are employees rewarded or chastised for pointing out problems in the way things are done?

A library administrator who wants to create a tactics-friendly environment should look for ways to create clear channels for communication and relationship-building in the organization. These channels should be both formal and informal, in person and asynchronous. To keep in-person discussions positive and on topic, authors Lois Kelly and Carmen Medina (2014) suggest listening carefully to others' opinions, avoiding "why" questions, and speaking last—a tactic that creates room for others to participate while providing you with the most complete picture before you jump in.

Administrators can also model ways to communicate new ideas to staff who might be resistant to or uncertain about them. This doesn't mean creating a heavy, top-down hierarchical message. To help build buy-in for new ideas, Kelly and Medina suggest positioning "the new idea as integral to what people deeply believe in about the organization—what they want to achieve, be known for, or value" (49). So if you want to experiment with new signage or classification and your organization values making the collection accessible to users, frame the new idea around how the new system will improve findability. People are more likely to be able to accept change if they see how it fits into their existing values.

Kelly and Medina also suggest painting a picture of the new idea with concrete examples rather than generalities—explaining "Here's how a new mother will find storytime class schedules with the changes in the foyer," or "History faculty will click here to browse new books every month," rather than saying, "The proposed changes will improve user experience." The authors emphasize the need to be upbeat and concise—to avoid wasting people's time with meandering or vague ideas and to clearly show how the idea will work (maybe even with pictures). They also caution against getting caught in the weeds, at least during the initial introductory phase for a new idea: "It's vital to show the gap between the ideal and the current state and briefly highlight the milestones for closing the gap. Avoid going into detail. If you're explaining, you're losing" (51).

Choosing Partnerships and Building Relationships

Most tactical interventions benefit from some kind of partnership—and most libraries benefit from thoughtful partnerships with other organizations. If your tactically minded staff bring you proposals that would benefit from others' contributions, you have some things to think about. Does a partnership with another entity make sense? If so, what form should that partnership take? How should it be recorded or formalized? Who should make the overture, and how should the relationship deepen and grow?

As your project builds support and momentum, it will be important to build clear communication channels with all partners. It's also important to realize that most organizations have distinct work cultures and that your library's culture might not perfectly align with that of even another library or cultural organization.

To help bridge cultural and personal divides, Kelly and Medina encourage administrators to create opportunities for staff to get to know each other a little outside the context of the immediate work project. "A good first step is getting to know people as people and giving them an opportunity to get to know you" (40). The authors recommend structuring a way for people to go out to lunch or coffee together and talk across institutional divides—not about the project but about life in general. These kinds of conversations build understanding and empathy, which are not only important in any workplace but key to negotiating for new ideas.

Bragging—A Right and a Duty

We may not like it, but studies show it's true: most librarians are introverted, cerebral types. A 1992 study of 1,600 librarians' Myers-Briggs personality types found that most were introverted and had a preference for analysis and critique (Thinking) over intuition and insight (Feeling) as a way of making decisions. Following up on those findings in 1995, Scherdin and Beaubien comment that "introverts do not show their best side to the outside world. Although a well-developed Introvert can deal ably with the Extroverted world when necessary, he/she works best with the reflective world of ideas" (37).

This characteristic can create a challenge for library leaders, who must voice the organization's values both internally and to the outside world. Library administrators don't brag just about their own accomplishments (or they shouldn't). They articulate the whole organization's excitement, pride, and momentum toward a shared vision. Library leaders, who have visibility and recognition that others in the organization lack, are effectively charged with bragging for those who can't brag for themselves.

But bragging can be tough to do right. As Jonathan Berman and his colleagues put it in their research study on bragging, "There exists a strong norm to be modest about prosocial behavior" (2015, 90). In other words, most Americans don't want to hear you toot your own horn, even if you've done something really great.

Matthew Hutson, writing for the *Atlantic*, recommends dodging negative consequences by finding someone to do your bragging for you—in studies in which listeners knew that a third party was paid to praise a research subject, they still rated the subject higher (and the boasting less annoying) than when the subject praised himself (2016). Hutson also recommends introducing the topic you want to boast about more generally because listeners typically respond better to an indirect discussion of accomplishment rather than a simple, unambiguous brag.

In a library context, there are a few ways you can reframe "bragging" in a positive light, especially when you're speaking for your whole organization. Recognizing employee success, sharing lessons learned, and promoting the organization are all completely valid ways to brag about your organization's successes.

Recognizing success—for individuals and departments as well as the organization overall—is critical to keeping staff engaged. Writing for the *Harvard Business Review*, Fortune 500 CEO Lou Solomon reported the number one reason one thousand U.S. employees criticized their bosses: "not recognizing employee achievements" (2015, 3). We just discussed some ways to recognize staff success internally and one-on-one, but remember that for bigger projects, you should up the recognition ante. Praising successful projects at higher-level functions such as all-staff meetings or in outward-facing venues such as the library newsletter or annual report are all good ways to reward engaged employees and boost morale. As a library leader, you have the power to magically transform boasting (something many people dislike) into praise (something almost everyone likes).

Sharing news of your library's success isn't just good for employee morale. It's also an important way to get the word out about something that worked well for you. Each of the case studies in this book shares valuable ideas that can help others replicate or adapt the project. None of them would be as useful if they hadn't been published in some way. And tactical projects are particularly vulnerable to vanishing under the radar because they're by definition small-scale, short-term, and often ephemeral.

Finally, if your library tries something tactical and it works out, sharing the news can boost the image of your organization and even the profession overall. That, in turn, can inspire more library administrators to take the leap off the ledge and devote some resources to a tactical project. The Cleveland Public Library's high-profile temporary art installations may not be replicable in libraries without big arts endowments, but the delight they bring to neighbors and passersby reflect well on public libraries in general. The Maricopa County Library's ShelfLogic system isn't for everyone, but when the project made the *New York Times*, it showed that plenty of everyday people care about how libraries work. If your own project doesn't have easy stats to share, consider how the L!brary Initiative organizers framed their successes around not only the number of libraries redesigned or the amount of money raised but also increased library awareness, new relationships, and changes in attitudes among families, teachers, and even the architects and designers who worked on the project. Sharing tactical successes helps build the positive perception of libraries as creative, engaged organizations.

TWELVE STEPS TO BECOMING A TACTICAL LIBRARY INTERVENTIONIST

B Y NOW YOU MIGHT BE GETTING INSPIRED TO TAKE ON A TACtical intervention in your own workplace. If you read nothing else, this section of the book should help get you launched by boiling everything down to a dozen easy-to-follow steps. Review this list before you start, and use it to help your tactical dreams come true.

1. **Start small.** Light, cheap, and quick—those are the watchwords of the tactical interventionist. Remember that although tactics are often guided by strategy (more on that later in this chapter), they're a different animal. Tactics are nimble, ingenious, creative, lightweight, and often temporary or ephemeral. They're responsive and agile. That means they can (and should) be smaller, cheaper, and quicker than large-scale, long-term strategic projects. There are obvious upsides to taking a tactical approach—you can get lots done for less, on a shorter time line. There are also downsides—your projects might not be as ambitious, as lasting, or as effective as you'd like. But remember that in the world of tactical interventions, starting small allows you to try things you otherwise couldn't.

A modest pilot project is usually better than no project at all—and sometimes it's just what you need to gain support for something bigger.

2. **Set achievable goals.** Big problems are important but overwhelming. If the problem you seek to fix is something like "People don't use their public libraries enough," and the goal you set is "Get people to use public libraries more," you're likely to be undone by both the vagueness and scope of your ideas. Remember the difference between strategy and tactics, and let strategy take care of the really big-picture stuff. Use tactics to break down the big problems into smaller, more manageable pieces that you can tackle individually. Think of the Green Guerrillas in 1970s New York City—faced with the collapse of the city's economy and infrastructure, they focused on salvaging a single abandoned lot. That lot-turned-garden became an exemplar of what was possible and helped build an international movement for green space and urban sustainability.

3. **Grow if it makes sense . . . or stay small if it makes sense.** In many ways, our modern world teaches us that "bigger is better." Bigger houses, bigger cars, bigger budgets, bigger library buildings—we can be forgiven for occasionally assuming that the goal of every project is to grow, grow, grow. But for tactical interventionists, small can be beautiful. It's up to you to decide whether your small tactical project is well served by growing, or if it makes more sense to keep its scope tightly focused. That's a decision you might want to make at the outset when you articulate your goals. The Astoria Scum River Bridge is an example of a tactical project that started small and stayed small . . . and still accomplished something noteworthy. EveryLibrary is an example of a tactical project that was always intended to grow big, so that it could serve libraries all across the country. Don't feel that your project has to grow in order to be successful. Decide for yourself what your benchmarks will be, and concentrate on measuring and sharing them.

4. **Talk to everybody.** As we've seen, the most successful tactical interventions demonstrate strong relationships with partners, close ties to locals affected by the issue at hand, and a shared sense of ownership. Especially for projects with longer time lines and more ambitious goals, transparency and openness are key. Talking to people about your project allows you to test ideas and gauge responses, collect early feedback, modify and improve your ideas, and catch problems before they get too big. It also allows you to drum up enthusiasm and collect skills, relationships, and other resources that you might need (and not already have). Lois Kelly and Carmen Medina call this process "socializing" your idea, the same way you might socialize a new pet. "The way to bring an idea to life is by helping people see the value in the idea for them and asking them to be part of the effort. Socialize your idea with many people, and work hard to get those one or two first followers who will take ownership and start to talk about it with others" (2014, 54). The more people you bring on board with your ideas, the broader your base of support and the more resilient and resourceful your project will be.

5. **Engage partners.** You're already talking to everybody—isn't that enough? Sorry, probably not. It's one thing to make sure that people know about your project. It's another to invite them to join you and to make space for them to do so. Give some thought to whom you're trying to reach or serve with your project and then consider how you can include them in it. (Bear in mind that some of those relationships may need to be sanctioned by library administrators.) A relatively modest project, such as the Forest Park Library's temporary "EXPLORE" signage, might only include the community late in the game. A more ambitious project, such as Newmarket's plan for the seasonal open-air Story Pod, requires more complex and long-term partnerships with funders, municipal employees, the public library system, and city government. Don't expect that simply telling people about your project is enough to gain their contribution. Decide who your essential partners are and invite them clearly and early in the process—and then prepare to be flexible if things change.

6. **Value experimentation, iteration, and incubation.** Tactical projects can be valuable testbeds for new ideas and methods—and sometimes that's enough. Remember that tactics don't have to change the world. Sometimes they just have to get people thinking in new ways, or show the full range of possibilities. Sometimes they just need to test out ideas at a lower price point before you launch a major project. Experimentation and iteration can be valuable recruiting tools, too. The Magdeburg Open-Air Library proponents spent time building a full-scale beer-crate replica of the library that they eventually aimed to build for real—and in doing so, they stoked the enthusiasm of locals and showed their eventual funders that they could pull the project off.

7. **Value relationships and social capital.** It's easy to overlook the enormous worth and potential of relationships. After all, there's no balance sheet that reflects who will take your calls or how many people you can bring out to a 7 p.m. event on a Tuesday. There's no way to quantify how your standing has improved in your local arts, cultural, or business community as a result of your outreach work. But relationships are critical to getting things done, both within our own organizations and with our partners. How people think about the library affects how they use it, talk about it, and vote about its interests. And whether or not we can put a number on social capital, tactical interventions both depend on it and are good at fostering it. Find ways to reflect that reality in your goal-setting and assessment—consider how the L!brary Initiative reports alternative metrics such as new partnerships established, funding sources secured, attitudes improved, and awareness increased about the importance of school libraries among the architects, elected officials, fund-raisers, and other partners who worked on the project.

8. **Value delight.** Most of the time, nobody's paying tacticians to do the serious work of improving a less-than-perfect situation. But that doesn't mean that tactical interventions have to be grim, dutiful, or preachy. Indeed, because tactics are so lightweight and low-threshold compared to strategy, they offer tremendous opportunities for

creativity and freedom of expression. Add in the tendency of tactics to playfully and provocatively tweak the status quo, and you may have a recipe for a passion project—something that will balance hard work with delight for both the interventionist and the community. Consider the cheeky dedication plate on the Astoria Scum River Bridge, or the brightly colored snails and meerkats that the Cleveland Public Library installed around its perimeter as part of the See Also arts project. Delight, charm, and humor can help fuel a project despite a low budget, and they can help create a friendly welcome to engage the rest of the community.

9. **Allow fruitful disruption.** Early on, we discussed some of the things that tactical urbanism isn't—including a chaotic upheaval of all order and hierarchy. And we've talked about how tacticians need to build bridges, form partnerships, and value relationships and goodwill. But a little upheaval can be a good thing. We've seen that most tactical interventions happen because of a problem or a need for change. Because they're so nimble and quick to try, tactics are particularly good for helping kick-start new ways of thinking. They can use humor and delight to shake things up without alienating stakeholders. And because they're low-threshold, they can give a voice (and some responsibility) to folks at the grassroots level, even in organizations with strict hierarchies. Consider the LibraryBox, which lets nonsystems librarians do an end run around dysfunctional or nonexistent wireless networks in schools and other settings. Sometimes a little disruption is a good thing.

10. **Be a respectful gadfly to the official power structure.** This is one of the stickiest areas of tactical intervention, especially if you're doing it from within an organization. When you meet with resistance or indifference to your ideas, it can be hard to walk the line between "productive dissenter" and "bad-mannered agitator." That line can vary from issue to issue, team to team, and day to day. If your goal is truly to better a situation and you choose a tactical approach, you must commit to remaining respectful regardless of how passionate you may feel. Remember that in taking the role of gadfly,

your goal is not truly to nettle and annoy individuals but to offer positive alternatives and urge a better path forward. Consider both the potential benefits of change and the weighty, often costly investments in the status quo—and the human administrator caught between the two. Thinking of (and clearly framing) your proposed intervention as a pilot project, experiment, incubator, or laboratory can help relieve pressure and resistance while showing how things can be done differently. In the spirit of tactical ingenuity, you might research how diplomats, politicians, and nonviolent leaders have made change happen through persistence, creativity, and offering ways for gatekeepers to "save face" while changing direction.

11. **Partner with the official power structure.** Where you meet with openness, receptivity, or even enthusiasm from the official power structure, your path is simpler. Remember that tactics are most powerful in partnership with strategy—similarly, tactical interventionists are most effective in partnership (or at least in agreement) with the existing power structure. If you can tap into official budget, staffing, communication, and other resources, you have that much less to organize on your own. You may want to draft a clear statement of understanding (e-mail may be sufficient depending on the context) of your project's goals and values to avoid scope creep, drift, or simple misunderstandings.

12. **Plan your exit strategy: sunset, persist, or transfer responsibility.** Just as you shouldn't assume that every tactical intervention needs to grow, grow, grow, you shouldn't assume that every project needs to carry on forever. Some projects will get better over time, while others only need to exist for a little while to make their mark. Think of Newmarket's Story Pod, which only emerges for a few months every year but still makes a lasting statement about the city's values and spirit. On the other hand, the ShelfLogic "Deweyless" classification scheme worked out so well that it made sense not just to keep it but to broaden its use permanently across the whole Maricopa County system. You might make some educated guesses at the start

of your project—will it be a short-term project or something that might persist for years? If it does continue, who will be responsible for it? Will it carry on in its original shape and scope, or will it change? How will you document changes, if they happen? How (and how often) will you assess it to see if it's still working and worth the investment?

TACTICAL FOLLOW-UPS: WHERE TO FIND MORE

THERE ARE PLENTY of places you can look for more tactical inspiration. Google "tactical urbanism" and you'll find a treasure trove of nonprofits, white papers, blogs, and websites. The sources listed here are highly curated and are some that you might not find as easily. Download a podcast, pick up a magazine, and get connected with urbanists, librarians, and placemakers thinking creatively about the world around us. Then go forth and practice tactics!

IN PRINT
Works That Work :
Magazine of Unexpected Creativity
https://worksthatwork.com
This small Dutch magazine (written in English) offers beautiful photography and short, thoughtful articles about ingenuity all over the world, from solar streetlamps for pennies a watt in Manila to high-fashion handbags repurposed as covert guerrilla gardening tools in London. The magazine offers an unusual distribution model to subscribers willing to tote a few copies along to far-flung locales: "If your travel plans coincide

with our delivery needs, you can help reduce the cost of shipping the magazine, making it more affordable for everyone, plus you get to meet super nice people, and you'll get a free copy of the latest issue as a thank-you."

IN AUDIO
Placemakers
www.slate.com/podcasts/
placemakers.html
Slate launched this new podcast in 2016, highlighting people making positive differences in the places where they live. If you're looking for more context for the idea of "placemaking" or want some inspiration in your workout, download the episode about Majora Carter's self-gentrification work in the South Bronx. Or pick from episodes about building better city bike-share programs or alternatives to suburban sprawl, or (just for fun) learn about George Leonidas Leslie, a trained architect who used his mastery of city and building systems to become the father of the modern bank heist.

Urbanism Speakeasy
www.urbanismspeakeasy.com/
Specifically pitched at laypeople who want to know more about urban design without getting a master's in public administration, Andy Boenau's weekly podcast is opinionated and accessible. Covering everything from bike advocacy to sprawl, Boenau talks to experts and activists about making cities more human-friendly and livable. Boenau also produced an Internet TV series called WalkLobby.TV, and he has a clear but amiable bias in favor of New Urbanist–style livable city design.

ON THE WEB
Library as Incubator
www.libraryasincubatorproject.org/
The Library as Incubator Project started as the class project of three intrepid MLIS students at the University of Wisconsin-Madison. Its focus is on the ways in which artists and librarians can collaborate and how libraries can provide space for the creation of artworks. Visit it for a blast of inspiration on opening up your library to new partnerships and ways of building decentralized ownership. As of this writing, the organizers were partway through a series called the Library Takeover program, "a project designed to commit library resources to groups of community members that want to make their ideas for free, open community events happen at the library."

IN PERSON
Open Engagement
http://openengagement.info/
Open Engagement is an annual conference for socially engaged artists founded by Jen Delos Reyes, associate director of the School of Art and Art History at the University of Illinois at Chicago. The concept might not sound relevant to tactical urbanism, but the topics often are. The 2015 keynote speaker was Rick Lowe, an artist, organizer, and MacArthur genius who founded Project Row House, which bought and restored dilapidated and low-cost nuisance properties in Houston, Texas, to create housing for low-income mothers and residency space for artists. In 2016 the keynote speaker was activist Angela Davis, and the program included sessions on anti-gentrification tools and city park design.

Urban Librarians Conference
www.urbanlibrariansconference.org/
Whether or not you work in an urban library, this one-day conference is a great way to mingle with other librarians and educators who value creativity and tactics. In 2016 keynote speaker R. David Lankes addressed the differences between complex and complicated problems, and in 2015 Lancelot Chase spoke about his work with Majora Carter's StartUp Box project in the South Bronx. Past presenters have included everyone from Patrick Sweeney (a librarian who uses a LibraryBox to carry digital materials up and down the California coast in his sailboat) to Sarah Houghton, director of the San Rafael (California) Public Library and the famous Librarian in Black.

9

SUMMING UP

ONGRATULATIONS! IF YOU'VE MADE IT ALL THE WAY THROUGH this book, you've covered a lot of ground. Together we've gotten our arms around the ungainly but lovable concept of tactical urbanism, then examined a few case studies to understand exactly what makes a project "tactical." After embracing the key characteristics of quick, cheap, and lightweight, we've also taken on board the importance of sharing ownership with a diverse group of stakeholders, valuing intangible benefits, and providing humor and delight. We've then launched ourselves into the world of libraries, where we've seen creative librarians and library staff use these same ideas to tackle complex and even wicked problems—or sometimes just to make the status quo a little better. After observing how libraries and cities share a lot of common ground, we've pondered the realistic demands and limits of tactical intervention, and spent a little time considering the special role of library leaders and administrators in fostering tactics-friendly cultures. Finally, we've boiled it all down to twelve simple steps to jump-start your own tactical intervention.

I hope you've found this book illuminating, inspiring, and maybe a little challenging. I also hope you'll keep looking for examples of tactical interventions in the world around you. There are plenty of other excellent tactical library projects that could have fit into this book, if only we had the room. Library for All, providing e-books to the developing world, is one that jumps to mind. So is Urban Libraries Unite, a grassroots organization of librarians who work together to provide better library services in cities. The trend of libraries hosting Wikipedia edit-a-thons is a great example of quick, low-cost, low-threshold tactics. Even the familiar one-city-one-book phenomenon is intriguing to consider through a tactical lens, as a means of radical engagement and relationship-building with the community.

I hope that as you learn more about these and other projects, you'll find yourself parsing them for the elements that make them successful. You might be surprised to see how much they have in common with each other, and how consistently they rely on the concepts we've discussed here. You might also be surprised at the power of tactics, and the wide range of things they can accomplish.

Finally, I hope that you'll find ways to bring a tactical mindset into your life, wherever and however it serves you best. I hope you'll value intangible benefits, build social capital, and plan for delight as well as practical outcomes. And if you have an idea for a great tactical project or know of one that really takes the cake, I'd love it if you shared. Publish, present, or send me an email. Let's keep showing that tactics work.

REFERENCES

American Library Association. n.d. "Return on Investment (ROI)." Text. *Libraries Matter.* www.ala.org/research/librariesmatter/taxonomy/term/129.

Appleton, Jay. 1996. *The Experience of Landscape.* Chichester, NY: Wiley.

ArchDaily. 2015. "Story Pod / Atelier Kastelic Buffey." *ArchDaily*, November 25. www.archdaily.com/777711/story-pod-atelier-kastelic-buffey.

Beale, Scott. 2006. "PARK(ing) Day 2006." *Laughing Squid*, September 20. https://laughingsquid.com/parking-day/.

Behance, Inc. 2009. "Encourage Daylighting." *99U by Behance*, January 20. http://99u.com/articles/5766/encourage-daylighting.

Bennett, Chuck. 2010. "No Ooze Is Good News." *New York Post*, January 28. http://nypost.com/2010/01/28/no-ooze-is-good-news/.

Berman, Jonathan Z., Emma E. Levine, Alixandra Barasch, and Deborah A. Small. 2015. "The Braggart's Dilemma: On the Social Rewards and Penalties of Advertising Prosocial Behavior." *Journal of Marketing Research (JMR)* 52 (1): 90–104. doi:10.1509/jmr.14.0002.

Bessette, Lee Skallerup. 2016. "The Unworkshop." *The University of Mary Washington Division of Teaching and Learning Technologies*, September 13. http://umwdtlt.com/the-unworkshop/.

Besson, Eric. 2013. "Election 2013: Voters Asked to Rededicate Library Funding toward Jail." *Times* (Houma, LA), November 13. http://www.houmatimes.com/news/election-voters-asked-to-rededicate-library-funding-toward-jail/article_d1cd291e-4bd9-11e3-acb2-001a4bcf887a.html.

Bozikovic, Alex. 2015. "Community in a Box: How Modern Design Is Helping Bring a Town Together." Globe and Mail, October 2. www .theglobeandmail.com/life/home-and-garden/architecture/new market-story-pod-blends-little-free-libraries-with-community -revival/article26635228/.

Brooklyn Public Library. 2015. "Participatory Art Project Opens Conversation on Transition in Brooklyn's Prospect Heights Neighborhood." September 30. www.bklynlibrary.org/media/press/participatory -art-project.

Brownlee, John. 2016. "Putting Leftover Urban Space to Use—as Crazily Shaped Soccer Fields." Fast Company, September 28. https://www .fastcodesign.com/3064132/putting-leftover-urban-space-to-use-as -crazily-shaped-soccer-fields.

Buscada. 2015. Intersection Prospect Heights. https://www.youtube.com/ watch?time_continue=26&v=ZipwRnbCCMo.

Cardon, Melissa S., Joakim Wincent, Jagdip Singh, and Mateja Drnovsek. 2009. "The Nature and Experience of Entrepreneurial Passion." Academy of Management Review 34 (3): 511–32. doi:10.5465/AMR.2009 .40633190.

Chan, Sewell. 2007. "Parking Lot in Dumbo Becomes a Public Plaza." City Room. http://cityroom.blogs.nytimes.com/2007/08/09/parking-lot-in -dumbo-becomes-a-public-plaza/.

Charles, Cassidy. 2012. "Is Dewey Dead?" Public Libraries Online, December 18. http://publiclibrariesonline.org/2012/12/is-dewey-dead/.

Chrastka, John. 2013. "Filling the Advocacy Gap: How Millions of Dollars Are at Stake on Ballots and What We're Doing about It | Advocates' Corner." Library Journal (April 3). http://lj.libraryjournal.com/2013/ 04/advocacy/filling-the-advocacy-gap-how-hundreds-of-millions -of-dollars-are-at-stake-for-libraries-on-local-ballots-and-what-were -doing-about-it/.

Christensen, Julia. 2008. Big Box Reuse. Cambridge, MA: MIT Press.

Civil Rights Project. n.d. "Choice without Equity: Charter School Segregation and the Need for Civil Rights Standards." The Civil Rights Project.

https://civilrightsproject.ucla.edu/research/k-12-education/
integration-and-diversity/choice-without-equity-2009-report.

Clearleft. 2005. "Suffolk Libraries Design Sprint | Clearleft." http://
clearleft.com/made/suffolk-libraries-design-sprint.

Cook, David. 2014. "Metadata Management on a Budget." *Feliciter.*

Coombs, G. 2012. "Park(ing) Day." *Contexts* 11 (3): 64–65. doi:10.1177/
1536504212456186.

Cooper, Ginnie. 2010. "In the Interims (Cover Story)." *Library Journal*
(September): 1–6.

Disser, Nicole. 2014. "The Most Uncomfortable—but Necessary—Event
in Town Is Brooklyn Transitions: The Gentrification Series!"
Brooklyn Magazine, October 21. www.bkmag.com/2014/10/21/
the-most-uncomfortable-but-necessary-event-in-town-is-brooklyn
-transitions-the-gentrification-series/.

DUMBO Improvement District. 2012. "What's Happening at the Pearl
Street Triangle?" *Dumbo,* June 14. http://dumbo.is/blogging/
whats-happening-at-the-pearl-street-triangle/.

———. 2015. "Pearl Street Triangle." *Dumbo*, May 28. http://dumbo.is/
hometo/pearl-street-triangle/.

dumbonyc. 2010. "Pearl Street Triangle 'Ideas Competition.'" *Dumbo
NYC*, June 22. http://dumbonyc.com/blog/2010/06/22/pearl-street
-triangle-ideas-competition/.

Eppink, Jason. 2010. "Astoria Scum River Bridge." *Vimeo.com.* https://
vimeo.com/10680837.

EveryLibrary.org. n.d.a. "Artist In Residence Program." *EveryLibrary.*
http://everylibrary.org/artist-residence-program/.

———. n.d.b. "Our Library Communities—EveryLibrary History."
EveryLibrary. http://everylibrary.org/library-communities
-everylibrary-history/.

———. n.d.c. "Rapid Response Fund." *EveryLibrary.* http://everylibrary.
org/rapid-response-fund/.

———. n.d.d. "What We Do." *EveryLibrary.* http://everylibrary.org/how
-we-help-libraries/.

Fister, Barbara. 2010. "The Dewey Dilemma." *Library Journal* (May 20). http://lj.libraryjournal.com/2010/05/public-services/the-dewey -dilemma/.

Flegenheimer, Matt. 2013. "Turning the City's Wheels in a New Direction." *New York Times*, December 29. www.nytimes.com/2013/12/30/ nyregion/turning-the-citys-wheels-in-a-new-direction.html.

Flood, Joe. 2010. "Why the Bronx Burned." *New York Post*, May 16. http:// nypost.com/2010/05/16/why-the-bronx-burned/.

Fox, Jeremy C. 2012. "Chinatown Celebrates Opening of New Community Library." *Boston.com*, April 24. http://archive.boston.com/yourtown/ news/downtown/2012/04/chinatown_celebrates_opening_0.html.

Frishberg, Hannah. 2016. "Farmers Market Bringing Locally Sourced Food to the Pearl Street Triangle This Summer." *Dumbo NYC*, June 2. http://dumbonyc.com/blog/2016/06/02/dumbo-farmers-market -brooklyn-pearl-street-triangle-hours/.

Furr, Nathan. 2011. "How Failure Taught Edison to Repeatedly Innovate." *Forbes.com*, June 9. www.forbes.com/sites/nathanfurr/2011/06/09/ how-failure-taught-edison-to-repeatedly-innovate/#6406a74138f5.

Gadanho, Pedro. 2014. *Uneven Growth: Tactical Urbanisms for Expanding Megacities*. New York: The Museum of Modern Art.

Goldberg, Beverly. 2012. "An Interview with John Chrastka." *American Libraries* (October 10). https://americanlibrariesmagazine.org/2012 /10/10/an-interview-with-john-chrastka/.

Gordinier, Jeff. 2016. "South Bronx Gets High-End Coffee; Is Gentrification Next?" *New York Times*, May 31. www.nytimes.com/2016/06/01/ dining/coffee-shops-south-bronx.html?module=Endslate&region= SlideShowTopBar&version=EndSlate&action=Click&contentCollection =Food&slideshowTitle=If%20You%20Brew%20It%20 . . . &currentSlide =Endslate&entrySlide=1&pgtype=imageslideshow.

Gordner, Trey. 2016. "KOIOS: Library Visibility across the Web." March 21. https://www.newschallenge.org/challenge/how-might-libraries -serve-21st-century-information-needs/evaluation/koios-library -visibility-across-the-web.

Green Guerrillas. n.d. "Our History." *Green Guerrillas*. www.greenguerillas .org/history.

Grynbaum, Michael M. 2011. "Janette Sadik-Khan, Lionized and Criticized." *New York Times*, March 4. www.nytimes.com/2011/03/06/ nyregion/06sadik-khan.html.

Hutson, Matthew. 2016. "How to Boast on the Sly." *Atlantic*, May. www .theatlantic.com/magazine/archive/2016/05/how-to-boast-on-the -sly/476373/.

Innovation Academy. 2016. "University of Florida: Students Sprint to the Catalyst Showcase." *Sprint Stories*, August 29. https://sprintstories .com/university-of-florida-students-sprint-to-the-catalyst-showcase -a0859030cd71.

Ippoliti, Cinthya. 2016. "From Zero to Sixty in under One Year: A Practical Approach to Building New Programs and Services, Managing Change, and Embracing Innovation as a New Library Administrator." *Library Leadership and Management* 31 (1). https://journals.tdl.org/ llm/index.php/llm/article/view/7193.

Kelly, Lois, and Carmen Medina. 2014. *Rebels at Work*. First edition. Sebastopol, CA: O'Reilly Media.

Kolleeny, Jane. 2005. "Robin Hood Foundation Library Initiative." *Bloomberg.com*, November 21. https://www.bloomberg.com/news/ articles/2005–11–20/robin-hood-foundation-library-initiative.

Lametti, Daniel, and Katy Waldman. 2012. "How an Abandoned Wal-Mart Became an Award-Winning Public Library." *Slate.com*, July 7. www .slate.com/blogs/browbeat/2012/07/07/abandoned_walmart_in _mcallen_texas_becomes_an_award_winning_public_library _how_big_box_stores_are_becoming_public_spaces_.html.

Lapowski, Issie. 2014. "Urban Onshoring: The Movement to Bring Tech Jobs Back to America." *WIRED*, November 4. https://www.wired .com/2014/11/urban-onshoring/.

Lau, Debra. 2002. "Gotham's Grand Vision." *Library Journal* (March 1). http://lj.libraryjournal.com/2002/03/ljarchives/gothams-grand-vision/.

LaVallee, Andrew. 2007. "Discord over Dewey." *Wall Street Journal*, July 20, sec. Technology. www.wsj.com/articles/SB118340075827155554.

"Leader of the PAC." 2014. *Library Journal* (March 10). http://lj.library journal.com/2014/03/people/movers-shakers-2014/john-chrastka -movers-shakers-2014-advocates/#_ .

Lee, Denny. 2001. "Friends of a Celebrated Garden Don't View a Pathway as Progress." *New York Times*, June 10. www.nytimes.com/2001/06 /10/nyregion/neighborhood-report-east-village-friends-celebrated -garden-don-t-view-pathway.html.

Lesneski, Traci. 2011. "Big Box Libraries: Beyond Restocking the Shelves with Books." *New Library World* 112 (9/10): 395–405. doi:http://dx.doi .org.libproxy.uoregon.edu/10.1108/03074801111181996.

Lindsey, Joe. 2015. "This Woman Built 400 Miles of Bike Lanes in New York City." *Bicycling*, December 31. www.bicycling.com/culture/ advocacy/this-woman-built-400-miles-of-bike-lanes-in-new-york -city.

Lowery, Wesley. 2014. "Young Protesters March for a Library in China-town." *BostonGlobe.com*, January 18. https://www.bostonglobe.com/ metro/2014/01/18/young-protesters-march-for-library-chinatown/ 6qGw3CWeYxh4H11aQCB3hP/story.html.

Luther, Elaine, and Alicia Hammond. 2016. "Exploring Public Art at the Forest Park Public Library." *Library as Incubator Project*, May 25. www.libraryasincubatorproject.org/?p=17093.

Lydon, Michael, Dan Bartman, Ronald Woudstra, and Arwash Khawar-zad. 2015. *Tactical Urbanism: Short Term Action || Long Term Change*. Washington, DC: Island Press. http://issuu.com/streetplans collaborative/docs/tactical_urbanism_vol_2_final.

Lydon, Mike, Dan Bartman, Tony Garcia, Russ Preston, and Ronald Wouldstra. 2017. "Tactical Urbanism 2: Short-Term Action, Long-Term Change." *Issuu*. Accessed January 7. https://issuu.com/street planscollaborative/docs/tactical_urbanism_vol_2_final/1.

MacDonald, Lawrence, and Todd Moss. 2014. "Building a Think-and-Do Tank (SSIR)." July 11. https://ssir.org/articles/entry/building_a_think _and_do_tank.

Maricopa County District Library. n.d. "ShelfLogic." http://mcldaz.org/ custom/shelflogic.aspx.

Mattern, Shannon. 2012. "Little Libraries and Tactical Urbanism." *Places*, 22. https://placesjournal.org/article/marginalia-little-libraries-in -the-urban-margins/.

McLemee, Scott. 2011. "Guerrilla Librarians in Our Midst." https://www .insidehighered.com/views/2011/11/02/essay-librarians-occupy -movement.

Mediati, Nick. 2015. "Pew Survey Shows 68 Percent of US Adults Now Own a Smartphone." *PCWorld*, November 1. www.pcworld.com/ article/2999631/phones/pew-survey-shows-68-percent-of-americans -now-own-a-smartphone.html.

MSR Meyer, Scherer and Rockcastle. n.d. "Denton Public Library North Branch." *MSR Architecture, Interiors, and Urban Design.* http:// msrdesign.com/project/denton-public-library-north-branch-2/.

Naparstek, Aaron. 2007. "City Launches 'Public Plaza Initiative' at DUMBO Pocket Park." *Streetsblog New York City*, August 10. http:// nyc.streetsblog.org/2007/08/10/city-launches-public-plaza-initiative -at-dumbo-pocket-park/.

Neuman, William. 2008. "Closing on Broadway: Two Traffic Lanes." *New York Times*, July 11. www.nytimes.com/2008/07/11/nyregion/ 11broadway.html.

New York City Department of Education. n.d. "NYC Data." http://schools .nyc.gov/Accountability/data/default.htm.

New York City Department of Parks and Recreation. n.d. "Start a Garden." www.greenthumbnyc.org/start_a_garden.html.

New York City Department of Transportation. 2015. "New York City 12-Hour Midtown Bicycle Count." www.nyc.gov/html/dot/downloads/ pdf/midtown-cycling-counts.pdf.

Nowviskie, Bethany. 2011. "A Skunk in the Library." *Bethany Nowviskie*, June 28. http://nowviskie.org/2011/a-skunk-in-the-library/.

O'Connell, Kim A. 2013. "Newest Urbanism." *Architect* 102 (7): 38–40.

Online Computer Library Center. 2013. "From Awareness to Funding: A Study of Library Support in America." August 9. https://www.oclc .org/en-CA/reports/funding.html.

Perera, Srianthi. 2013. "Gilbert Library Slowly Turns Cataloging Page." *AZ Central*, June 13. http://archive.azcentral.com/community/gilbert/ articles/20130612gilbert-library-slowly-turns-cataloging-page.html.

Rebar Group. 2012. "About PARK(ing) Day." http://parkingday.org/ about-parking-day/.

Reese, Terry. 2013a. "About MarcEdit." Text. *MarcEdit Development*, March 14. http://marcedit.reeset.net/about-marcedit.

———. 2013b. "About the Author." Text. *MarcEdit Development*, March 14. http://marcedit.reeset.net/about-the-author.

Reid, Ian. 2016. "The 2015 Public Library Data Service: Characteristics and Trends." Annual report. *Counting Opinions*. https://storage .googleapis.com/co_drive/Documents/PLDS/2015PLDSAnnual ReportFinal.pdf.

Richardson, Adam. 2010. "Considering a Skunk Works? Think Again." September 13. https://hbr.org/2010/09/considering-a-skunk-works -thin.

Rosenfield, Karissa. 2014. "New York Public Library Scraps Foster-Designed Renovation Plans." *ArchDaily*, May 8. www.archdaily .com/504584/new-york-public-library-scraps-renovation-plans/.

Sadik-Khan, Janette. 2016. "About." *Janette Sadik-Khan*. www.jsadikkhan .com/about.html.

Scherdin, Mary Jane, and Anne K. Beaubien. 1995. "Shattering Our Stereotype: Librarians' New Image." *Library Journal* 120 (12): 35–38.

Schneekloth, Lynda H., and Robert Shibley. 1995. *Placemaking: The Art and Practice of Building Communities*. New York: Wiley.

Seattle Public Library. n.d. "CEN Building Facts." www.spl.org/locations/ central-library/cen-building-facts.

Segarra, Marielle. 2015. "Author Interview: Tactical Urbanism." *Keystone Crossroads*, May 20. http://crossroads.newsworks.org/index.php/local/keystone-crossroads/82074-author-interview-tactical-urbanism.

Sheir, Rebecca. n.d. "Self-Gentrifying in the Bronx." *Slate Magazine.* www.slate.com/podcasts/placemakers/can_self_gentrification_remake_hunts_point_this_bronx_native_says_yes.html.

Solomon, Lou. 2015. "The Top Complaints from Employees about Their Leaders." *Harvard Business Review* (June): 2–5.

Street Lab. n.d. "Storefront Library (2009–10)." www.bostonstreetlab.org/projects/storefront-library/.

Subramanian, Sushma. 2013. "Google Took Its 20% Back, But Other Companies Are Making Employee Side Projects Work for Them." *Fast Company*, August 19. https://www.fastcompany.com/3015963/google-took-its-20-back-but-other-companies-are-making-employee-side-projects-work-for-them.

Vallerand, Robert, and Nathalie Houlfort. 2003. "Passion at Work: Towards a New Conceptualization." In *Emerging Perspectives on Values in Organizations*, 175–204. IAP.

Vogel, Thomas. 2015. "Artist, Library Spell-Out Path to Public Art." *Forest Park Review*, July 21. www.forestparkreview.com/News/Articles/7-21-2015/Artist,-library-spell_out-path--to-public-art/.

Whyte, William Hollingsworth. 1988. *City: Rediscovering the Center.* First edition. New York: Doubleday.

Wills, Heather. 2003. "An Innovative Approach to Reaching the Non-Learning Public: The New Idea Stores in London." *New Review of Libraries and Lifelong Learning* 4 (1): 107–20. doi:10.1080/1468994042000240250.

Winston, Andrew S. 2014. *The Big Pivot: Radically Practical Strategies for a Hotter, Scarcer, and More Open World.* Boston: Harvard Business Review Press.

Wong, Alia. 2016. "Where Books Are All but Nonexistent." *Atlantic*, July 14. www.theatlantic.com/education/archive/2016/07/where-books-are-nonexistent/491282/.

Wu, Chiahuei, and Sharon Parker. 2011. "Proactivity in the Workplace: Looking Back and Looking Forward." In *The Oxford Handbook of Positive Organizational Scholarship*, 84–96. Oxford, UK: Oxford University Press.

INDEX